Lord
Shaftesbury

Lord Shaftesbury

A PORTRAIT

by

Florence M. G. Higham

S.C.M. PRESS

56 Bloomsbury Street, London

First published March 1945

Distributed in Canada by our exclusive agents
The Macmillan Company of Canada Limited
70 Bond Street, Toronto

PRINTED IN GREAT BRITAIN BY
NORTHUMBERLAND PRESS LIMITED
GATESHEAD ON TYNE

Contents

I will not cease from mental fight,
  Nor shall my sword sleep in my hand,
Till we have built Jerusalem
  In England's green and pleasant land.
WILLIAM BLAKE, 1799.

Every child should find itself a member of a family housed
with decency and dignity, so that it may grow up as a
member of that basic community in a happy fellowship,
unspoilt by underfeeding or overcrowding, by dirty and drab
surroundings or by mechanical monotony of environment.
WILLIAM TEMPLE, Archbishop of Canterbury,

November 1941.

There is neither hope nor strength, nor comfort, nor peace,
but in a virtuous, a wise and an understanding people.
ANTHONY ASHLEY COOPER, Lord Ashley,
  (subsequently Earl of Shaftesbury), February 1843.

Prelude: 1885

IT was raining. The procession made its way through crowded streets towards the Abbey. In Parliament Street, delegates from innumerable societies waited behind their banners to join it as it passed. But despite bands and banners it was a sad occasion, for those who watched were thinking of a friend whom they would not see again. They stood side by side on the pavement, at one for a brief moment in their love for a man who had loved them all; and then they went their different ways, peers of the realm and Piccadilly flower-girls; black-coated clerks and waifs from the London streets; seamstresses and chimney-sweeps and statesmen and clergymen; the costermongers who played the band and the boys from H.M.S. *Arethusa*. Thus London paid its tribute to the seventh Earl of Shaftesbury. Next day his body was laid to rest at Wimborne St. Giles, the home of his forefathers. But the spirit of the man, the memory of eighty years of unfaltering service, lived on in the hearts of thousands, as it still lives to-day in the Shaftesbury Homes, in the training-ships on the Thames, in the housing estates of which he was the pioneer, in the welfare work and legal restrictions that ease the path of young people in industry, in the enlightened treatment of the insane and the work of the Ministry of Health, and in the belated realization by Christian people that every man has an equal right to freedom from want and fear.

Anthony Ashley Cooper, whom the world knew as Lord Ashley until his fiftieth year and who then succeeded his father as seventh Earl of Shaftesbury, dallied as a youth with the idea of studying science, but knew in his heart that his name and his inheritance marked him down for politics. In this sphere he had great and legitimate ambitions. He did not lack ability or influence or opportunity. He needed only to be somewhat more adaptable, rather more conven-

7

tional in his regard for party ties, a little less truly himself, to have been a leader of the Tory party. But one by one he put these ambitions behind him. On his twenty-seventh birthday he wrote of his future career: " The first principle God's honour, the second man's happiness, the means prayer and unremitting diligence."[1] To this recipe for a good life he remained faithful for fifty-odd years, deliberately devoting himself to helping others, by giving freely of himself to all who asked his aid and by inquiring ruthlessly into every injustice with which he came in contact. Voltaire wrote: ".The worst of the worthy sort of people is that they are such cowards. A man groans over wrong, he shuts his lips, he takes his supper and forgets." Shaftesbury cared passionately; he wept at the sight of a hungry child. Yet he never let his emotions impede his actions. The hungry children in the schoolyard, whose plight had made him weep, were fed within the hour on soup from his own kitchens; the gloomiest entries in his diary, to the pages of which he confided all his fears and anxieties, were followed at once by fresh assaults upon the walls of Jericho. He did wonders, through his faith and by sheer hard work, for there is no short cut to success even for miracle-workers.

It was his faith which enabled him to keep going. He was a totalitarian Christian. "I think," he said, "a man's religion, if it is worth anything, should enter into every sphere of life and rule his conduct in every relation." The glory of his life is this complete self-surrender to God. He was not a theologian and he did not talk much about his religion. He was a member of the Church and he endeavoured to be Christ's faithful soldier and servant to his life's end. The results were startling!

The new Jerusalem is not yet builded, and the sword that fell from Shaftesbury's hands needs in each generation to be wielded afresh. The men who work for God's kingdom to-day may have a wider vision, a deeper insight than he; they cannot have more courage nor more enduring patience.

[1] Quotations from the Diary are taken throughout from the three-volume *Life and Work of the 7th Earl of Shaftesbury* by Edwin Hodder [1887].

In their fight against the giants of ignorance and squalor and want, it may well be that they will stand or fall according to the measure of their kinship with Shaftesbury, whose work was the natural outcome of his faith that Christ meant it when He said, "Thou shalt love thy neighbour as thyself."

1

Early Years

MARIA MILLIS was a maid in the Duke of Marlborough's household. When her young mistress, the Duke's daughter, was married to Lord Ashley, Maria left Woodstock and came to London to act as housekeeper for the young couple at their home in Grosvenor Square. They were an exacting pair, but Maria was happy enough; she had her own reserves to draw upon; at Woodstock she had attended a church whose pastor was one of the new enthusiasts, an Evangelical as they were called, who had taught her to rely for joy and peace, not on outward circumstances nor on the things she herself might do, but on Christ's nearness, on a personal sense of His redeeming love. But when the children were born her heart was often heavy, for she watched them grow up in a home where they were never cherished. They dreaded their father's sternness and their mother's indifference, for she was busy with her empty, successful life as a woman of fashion while he devoted himself to public affairs, demanding of others the high standard of integrity he asked of himself but leaving no room in his heart for love or the grace of laughter. Three girls were born, and at last, on April 28th, 1801, a son—Anthony Ashley Cooper, heir to a great name.

Maria Millis adored the little boy. Whatever the future held for him of rank and fame, now he belonged to her. He was a solemn, sensitive child, moving quietly about the house lest his mother should be disturbed or his father angry. His parents would have been horrified if they had been told that they neglected their children. Their father maintained strict discipline and their mother taught them to be word-perfect in the Catechism. That was what she understood by religion. But Anthony was not very quick; with his sister Charlotte's aid he managed as best he could, but happiness came with the moment that found him back in the nursery, when he climbed on to Maria's knee and she taught him to say his prayers.

At the age of seven Anthony was sent away to school, to an establishment at Chiswick, suitable for the sons of gentlemen, fair enough in outward appearance but, beneath, a foul and horrible place. There he learnt Greek and Latin, and how beastly life can be. The first term was agony. He was homesick and afraid. But every night he said the prayer Maria had taught him and hoped that in the holidays she would be able to explain. And then he was told that she had died. When he went home his parents seemed more remote than ever, and the servants at times forgot the children's existence, so that more than once they went supperless to bed. When he grew up and heard of unhappy children, folk often tried to persuade him it was not so bad as it sounded. But this he never believed, for he remembered how desperately unhappy he himself had been.[1] One thing only helped him to endure, the thought of Maria's goodness, and the feeling that he could rely upon her teaching that Christ is a real and ever-present friend. He began to read more carefully the Bible which she had loved.

Fortunately, before long, matters improved. When he was twelve he went to Harrow, and here he was happy. Instead of an ordeal, it proved a release. He was able to learn and he loved finding out about things, and, for the rest, he could go his own way unmolested. Then, in the holidays, soon after the change of school, he went down for the first time to Wimborne St. Giles. Lord Ashley had succeeded his brother as Earl of Shaftesbury in 1811, and Anthony now was Lord Ashley and heir to St. Giles. He loved the place. He explored every corner of the estate and wandered through the surrounding villages; body and mind alike grew strong and straight again as congenial work and companionship at Harrow alternated with the beauty and tranquillity of holidays in Dorset.

His schoolmasters were not sure what to make of him. He was an unusual combination; practical, with a scientific

[1] Hammond's *Shaftesbury*, p. 3.

bent, and at the same time a dreamer. In his personality there were similar contradictions: shy and yet stubborn; remote yet enthusiastic; what would he make of life? One term an incident occurred which made them wonder still more. He had a Latin verse to write, and took for his subject a pond close by the school. In such classical phrases as he could muster, he declared it to be a common danger, a stagnant, unhealthy spot, a breeding-place for mosquitoes. The staff barely knew that the pond existed, but now they went to look for themselves. It was, in very fact, a pestilential spot and steps were taken at once to have it drained. Possibly, the more conventional members of the staff were somewhat perturbed: " A queer lad," they may have ruminated. " A boy of his age should mix more." But young Ashley seemed happy enough, even if he did like to wander off by himself.

On one such occasion, when he was nearly fifteen, Anthony met with a disturbing experience that he was never to forget. Walking down Harrow Hill, he checked himself suddenly to avoid collision with a group of drunken men coming out of a side street. They were carrying something which rolled from their shoulders as they swayed, cursing and bawling, round the corner, and to his dismay Anthony saw what it was, a cheap coffin, in which all that was left of some poor creature went its way to a pauper's grave, unaccompanied by any mourner, carried by these wretches whose hire had already been squandered in drink. The boy watched, stunned and horrified. " Good heavens," he cried, " can this be permitted simply because the man was poor and friendless? " That was the fact that angered and amazed him: that the mere absence of material possessions could inflict upon a person made in the image of God such indignity and such a miserable end. Something, he felt, must be done about it. He was only fourteen and could do nothing. Yet he would not always be young: one day it would be different. With cheeks still hot from the shame and embarrassment of the recent encounter, his knees still trembling and his heart pounding his side, he vowed that he would give his whole life to the service of the poor.

Ashley was still at Harrow when Waterloo was fought, and like every other boy he made Wellington his hero, regardless of the dark clouds of fear and repression that threatened the England of the Six Acts and Peterloo. He left Harrow in 1816 and spent two years in Derbyshire, in a clergyman's home, reading not very seriously for Oxford and exploring the green hills and stony dales of the Peak. Later he described them as two of the most misspent years of his life. Probably he was wrong. He was to endure to old age an existence of unremitting toil and continuous nervous strain, and it may well have been this period of lying fallow that established his bodily and mental health. Despite his religion, he often lacked serenity, battling with fits of depression, restless and worried till he lost himself in the next job: it was part of his inheritance from the first Earl of whom Dryden wrote:

> " *A fiery soul, which working out its way*
> *Fretted the pigmy body to decay*
> *And o'er-informed the tenement of clay.*"

But thanks to the interlude among the hills, the young Lord Ashley who entered Christ Church in October 1819 was master of himself, confident of his position in the world as a member of the ruling classes but equally conscious of the duties and responsibilities that position entailed.

At Christ Church he worked hard, and his industry, his modesty and his striking good looks won him the admiration of many though he made few intimate friends. He was tempted to choose an academic career, for there was much in it that appealed to him; the time for reflection and the satisfying character of facts, contrasted with the hurly-burly of unpredictable human relationships. But the vow he had made on Harrow Hill, the tradition of his family and of the aristocracy to which he belonged all claimed him for a more active life. He was intensely ambitious (that too was a heritage from the first Earl); but he was also diffident, and during the breathing space after Oxford he spent much time in anxious thought about the future. If he entered Parliament, could he hope to acquire enough influence to achieve the career of public usefulness of which he dreamed? He took it for granted that the service he hoped to render to humanity would be exercised through politics; and it was with his mind a jumble of quixotic visions, forebodings of failure and personal ambitions, that Ashley entered the Commons in 1826 as Tory member for Woodstock, a pocket borough of the Duke of Marlborough's.

Once inside Westminster he found it difficult to do anything at all. He did not speak easily and he was painfully conscious of his lack of any special ability. But he hated to be second-rate. There were times when he knew something should have been said, yet kept silent for fear he should say it badly. This was inverted pride and he chastised himself in the Diary. He must not fail. "The State may want me, wretched ass that I am." But others it appeared had a better opinion of him. In 1827, Wellington's Government fell when a group of young progressives under Canning's brilliant leadership broke away from their domineering chief. Canning asked Ashley to take office under him, but Ashley's admiration for the Duke had not lessened on personal acquaintance. So his first public act was to refuse Canning's offer and to ruin his own immediate chances of advancement. But Canning's tragic death a few months later put back the clock and Wellington returned to power. Early in 1828 Ashley accepted office as one of the Commissioners of the India Board of Control.

Now at last he was launched on his public career. He urged himself not to falter: "No fretting of the mind, no conceited nervousness for fear some sentence should fail in arrangement. . . . I must not dread coming down to the level of others." The chance to make his first important speech came soon. A Bill was introduced amending the law with regard to the treatment of lunatics. A commission of which Ashley was a member had been appointed in the previous year to enquire into the matter. Now he seconded the motion for leave to bring in the Bill. He was very nervous and not very audible, but his manner was straightforward and convincing, and a House whose appetite for oratory was jaded reacted favourably to Ashley's quiet presentation of the facts. The Bill was carried and Commissioners of Lunacy were appointed. Next year Ashley accepted the office of Chairman which, except for one brief interval, he held until his death.

His main interest in the next two years was India. He thanked God that he had been given a part in " this sublime guardianship of countless myriads", to whom England should give good government and a knowledge of the true religion. If ever man had the missionary spirit it was Ashley, and he had a somewhat naïve confidence that Indians had only to know the English better and to see their Christianity in practice to accept it fully. For his part he took his duties at the Board seriously, so much so that his fellow Commissioners soon realized that he was neither an ordinary nor a comfortable colleague. He refused to sign a despatch of which he disapproved; he made a study of native agriculture and urged various schemes for its development; he also insisted on discussing the unpopular subject of " suttee " and obtained its condemnation by the Board. Thorough in all things, he arranged to dine with the Directors of the East India Company: and found them pleasant and friendly, rather to his own surprise for he was still not used to meeting the middle-classes! To his delight he found that he could get on reasonably well with people. " Certainly I begin to think that I am popular with all classes," he wrote in the revealing pages of the Diary, " not vulgarly popular, but esteemed. . . . Thank God, I truckle for none, I hold a straight course and Providence blesses me above my deserts."[1]

It was a dangerous state of mind, but this new-won self-confidence was exactly what he needed for success in his next venture. For he fell in love! She was a member of a leading Whig family, a madcap beauty and the toast of

[1] Diary, under date November 13th, 1828.

the London season, and he was a serious and not very rich young man. In no respects was the match an appropriate one. But she also was in love. Her name was Emily Cowper. She was Earl Cowper's daughter and niece to Lord Melbourne, one of Canning's "progressives", who was now drifting, shrewd, cynical and imperturbably good-humoured, into the ranks of the Whigs. He was fond of his niece "Minnie" as they called her, but it needed more than her betrothal to a Tory to upset him. Other relatives were less considerate and described Ashley's family as "generally disliked" and "reputed mad". But all Lady Cowper cared about was that Minnie loved him and that he was a good young man. Over-serious, perhaps, he had only to feel gay on a January morning to worry as to why he was happy. But Minnie was content to seize happiness when it came her way. In June 1830 they were married and forty years of deepening devotion justified their choice.

They were not always easy years. There were ten children—six boys and four girls—and they were always short of money. The relations between Lord Ashley and his father grew very strained as their paths diverged, and the Earl made no increase in his son's allowance as the latter's commitments grew. Ashley lived simply, almost austerely, but he was always in debt. It was a comparative sort of poverty of course. He travelled regularly abroad in search of health, at first for himself and later for his children. But he never had spare cash to buy a new book (the sight of one was like a carrot to a donkey, he commented once), though an odd five pounds secreted for some emergency could usually be found to help anyone really in distress. But it was not material hardship nor the fact that Ashley was a bad business man that worried his wife. More exasperating were his alternating moods of self-confidence and intense depression; his utter disregard for convention or convenience if they impeded the success of the cause for which he was fighting; and his refusal to accept the good things of life. She really was cross with him for saying "No" when the Queen first offered him the

B

Order of the Garter! But Minnie remained her sunny self whatever his mood or his preoccupation. She never scolded. Many a woman has made a martyr of herself for her husband, not so many have refrained from telling him so. Through a life of varied experiences, visits to Windsor one day and to Whitechapel the next, of family joys and tragedy when death robbed them of children they adored, they grew nearer to each other, bound by their love and the religion of which they seldom spoke because it was part of their very being, no more to be argued about than the beauty of a spring day.

Ashley took little part in the crisis which broke upon England in 1830. In the General Election that year the Tories lost many seats, but despite his small majority, Wellington declared that he had no intention of introducing parliamentary reform, the issue upon which the election had been fought. He was as ready to die in the last ditch in politics as on the battlefield. "The House of Commons as at present constituted," he declared, "possesses the full and entire confidence of the country." Others begged to differ and the Duke was defeated. Upon his resignation the veteran Earl Grey became Prime Minister, and in March 1831 Lord John Russell introduced the Reform Bill.

Ashley was on the losing side in the forthcoming struggle. Reform to him was the thin end of the wedge that threatened the whole balance of life in England. When Russell's Bill was defeated and the House dissolved he stood without hesitation as anti-reform candidate for Dorset. He was returned, but there was a dispute about the election result which ran him into considerable expense, and the Duke's refusal to help him in the matter added to his vexation of spirit and to his sense of frustration. The old England he loved seemed to be falling to pieces about him, and the default of Wellington was symptomatic of the change. Of the new England—of the "dark satanic mills" and the people of Lancashire and Yorkshire struggling in the grip of the new industrialism to maintain some shreds of personal dignity—of all these changes which made Reform urgent

and necessary, he knew next to nothing. Yet while the
Whigs introduced their Bills in an atmosphere so intense
that civil war seemed near, others, approaching the problem from a different angle, attacked the worst evils of the
new machine age. In December 1831 a Yorkshireman,
Michael Sadler, introduced a Bill restricting the hours of
work in the factories for women and young persons to ten
hours per day. He made sufficient impression for a Committee of Enquiry to be appointed. Meanwhile the struggle
for Reform went on. When the third Bill passed the Commons, King William refused to co-operate by creating peers
to secure its passage through the Lords; Grey resigned and
Wellington, a soldier under orders, tried and failed to form
a government. Then the King gave in. Grey returned to
power, and in June 1832 the Reform Bill became law.

In the ensuing election, by one of those ironies in which
history delights, Michael Sadler, champion of the rights of
man, lost his seat at Hull to a brilliant opponent named
Thomas Babington Macaulay. There was dismay among
those who were working for the welfare of the men and
women in the factories. These pioneers, journalists, clergymen, operatives, mill-owners, were well organized on various
" Short Time Committees ". Yet without Sadler to act as their
spokesman at Westminster they were for the time being
impotent. Their representative in London was a pugnacious
clergyman, suitably named Bull. In their quandary, he recalled the efficient way Lord Ashley had supported the
cause of the lunatics in 1828. He recollected that Ashley
had written to him a few weeks earlier offering his services
in presenting petitions in Sadler's absence. Soon after the
House met, in February 1843, he approached Ashley and
asked him if he would take up the question of factory reform. It was a bold step, for the south-country aristocrat
knew little of conditions in the north and might fail them,
but Bull was a good judge of character, and after he had met
and talked with Ashley he had no hesitation in reporting to
the Short Time Committees that their new champion was as
" benevolent and resolute in mind as he is manly in person ".

Ashley for his part was amazed. His interest in the matter had only been roused by some articles in *The Times* that winter. He had missed the report of Sadler's committee in the previous August which disclosed a state of things that made action so imperative that the Short Time Committees feared lest the Government would sidetrack them by introducing an unsatisfactory measure of its own. They must secure a spokesman in Parliament, and Bull assured Ashley that there was no time to think it over. Eventually he gave him till next morning to decide.

Thus, suddenly and unawares, Ashley came to a turning-point in his life. If he agreed he cut himself adrift from the close party connection which, when the Tories returned to power, would secure him office and the chance to do great things. This new task would involve him in a lengthy struggle in which his new colleagues would be strangers and his former friends opposed to him. Moreover, the fear of doing things badly assailed him again, this time with a certain amount of justification. Yet it was a good cause, and he could be of use. He asked his wife's advice and she answered without hesitation: "It is your duty and the consequences we must leave. Go forward and to victory." Such an answer brooked no argument. Next morning he said " Yes " to Bull; and at the age of thirty-two set out upon his destined path and changed the whole direction of his life.

II

The Cry of the Children

A WAYFARER in London, at the end of the eighteenth century,
might often have paused to watch barges sailing down-
stream full of children, wizened, undersized creatures who
could only have come from the streets or from the workhouse or reformatory. Yet, wretched as they were, the
children could still smile, jostle one another, make faces at
the passer-by, challenge life with the invincible pluck and
impudence of the gutter-snipe of all ages. Happily they
did not know what lay before them, for they were destined
for the mills of Lancashire and Yorkshire. The wheels
turned, driven by water or by the new steam method, but
the output of the spinners and weavers depended on the
children who fed their machines, and upon that output
depended the mounting prosperity of England. Children
were needed, and in the London workhouses were unwanted
children, whose parents had often been thieves and vaga-
bonds. It was a kindness to apprentice such children to the
mills, introducing them to honest, industrious lives in place
of the filth and squalor of the streets. So, maybe, it seemed
to the sentimental onlooker as the barges sailed down the
Thames. And in the north they were used to it, to the
sight of misshapen youngsters, broken in body and spirit,
who were these same children after a few years of factory
life.

They worked as much as twelve or fifteen hours a day;
there was time neither for play nor schooling; they were
too tired to eat and sleep.

> And all day the iron wheels are droning,
>   And sometimes we could pray,
> " Oh, ye wheels " (breaking out in a sad moaning)
>   " Stop, be silent for to-day."[1]

[1] E. B. Browning: *The Cry of the Children.*

The war against Napoleon, by increasing the demand for textiles, aggravated the evil, yet as so often happens, it was under the shadow of war that the first efforts were made to build a fairer world. For thirty years before Ashley entered the struggle, others had been preparing the way. There were men of property who were also men of imagination and sympathy. There was Sir Robert Peel, father of a more famous son, a Lancashire mill-owner and member of Parliament. There was Robert Owen, a great man at making his dreams come true, and Nathaniel Gould, merchant, ready to back his dreamings with hard cash. To this little group of Manchester men belongs the honour of first persuading Parliament to take action (against all its economic principles) in the interests of the working classes. In 1802 a measure was passed restricting the hours of apprentice children to twelve hours a day and forbidding night work. To a large extent the Act remained a dead letter, but none the less it marked a triumphant breach in the ramparts of *laisser-faire*. But the battle was only begun. The apprentices were gradually replaced by free labour, unprotected by the law. When the mills had been worked by water they had been scattered up and down the countryside, but with the use of steam, a new evil emerged as the manufacturing towns of Lancashire and Yorkshire sprang into hideous yet vigorous being. The mills now grouped together near to the source of supply demanded labour and more labour, and from the impoverished countryside the families came in to answer the call, living in jerry-built back-to-back houses, built without thought of health or cleanliness to meet the growing need. The years of depression following the war made it hard for many of these immigrants to make ends meet, and in many cases it was dire necessity that first impelled the parents to let their youngsters work in the mill. It was a cruel business, this sacrifice to Mammon of the children of the poor. Many a rich man regretted it, but more took it for granted, and it kept few of them awake at nights, as the thought of Europe's starving children robs few of us of sleep to-day.

Happily some were different, men like Richard Oastler

whose heart was warm but whose pen was dipped in gall;
he had served his apprenticeship by fighting against slavery,
and in Yorkshire they called him "t'owd King". There was
John Fielden, a Sunday-school teacher who owned cotton
mills in Lancashire, and John Wood, worsted spinner of
Bradford, who had plenty of money to spend on a good
cause and never stinted it, and Joseph Brotherton, a factory
hand himself, who was determined that the misery he had
seen about him should by God's grace and man's endeavour
cease to darken the world. These men stood behind Peel
and Sadler and later Ashley, while the battle was fought out
over a space of thirty years. In 1819, Peel sponsored another
Bill, restricting the hours of work in the cotton mills for all
under sixteen years of age. In 1825 a further reduction of
hours took place and Sir John Hobhouse established a sixty-
nine-hour week for all workers under eighteen. Michael
Sadler's Bill in 1831 carried the crusade still further by
proclaiming the ten-hour day. It was not merely a humanitarian movement in the interests of the children. Indirectly
adults were also concerned. By lessening the time during
which the children who fed the machines could be employed,
a first step would be taken in the direction of Robert Owen's
eight-hour day, a triple division of the twenty-four hours
into work, sleep and leisure

After the long winter of the Napoleonic wars, there were
everywhere signs of life. In politics men demanded Reform;
in economics they cried for free corn; in the unmapped
realms of sociology they asked for a minimum of respect for
the personality of the poor in the creation of better conditions of labour and the provision of a certain amount of
leisure. At once there came a clash between these dimly
realized aspirations and the traditional theories of economics
and politics. Government existed to protect the lives and
property of the governed, it was concerned with the policing
and defence of the country, the maintenance of justice and
the raising of the necessary revenue. It was mainly a neg-
ative conception. Legislation, dealing with social rather
than purely political matters, was a new and somewhat

alarming idea. By what right should the State interfere
with the private lives of ordinary citizens? The Opposition
that seemed to Ashley so factious in the years to come were
right in seeing in the Factory Laws an innovation at least
as far-reaching as any Reform Bill, the thin end of the
wedge that would eventually produce the socialized state of
to-day.

Such were the problems and such the ferment of ideas
which faced young Ashley when he took up the cause of the
factory worker. Sadler's personal hopes of success had been
shattered by his defeat at the polls, and he died, worn out,
a couple of years later. But he had achieved one real success
in that last summer at Westminster. By obtaining the
appointment of the Committee of Enquiry, and by acting as
its Chairman and galvanizing it into speedy and effective
action, he secured the publication of its report in the summer of 1832. Men read with dismay the evidence of heart-
broken parents and of children too tired to stand upright,
whose deformed bodies and stunted minds bore witness to
the agony of their existence. Called in the small hours, too
sleepy to swallow their breakfast, they were pushed out into
the dark to spend twelve hours or more among the noise of
the machines. One witness said he had three children, the
youngest " going eight ". Sometimes they had worked in the
mill from three in the morning till after ten at night. A
year or so later Charles Dickens made the only possible
comment: " I went some weeks ago to Manchester and saw
the worst cotton mill. And then I saw the best. There was
no great difference between them." Faced with the facts of
Sadler's Committee, Ashley took up the cause in the spirit
of a crusader. He remained calm on the surface, a char-
acteristic which annoyed the hot-blooded Oastler, who wrote
to him on one occasion: " You, my Lord, must change your
heart for stone if you intend to be cool whilst you fight the
battle of the Factory Child." But the veneer was mislead-
ing. He was so made that the more he cared, the less he
displayed his feelings in public, yet it was in the battle of
the factory child that Ashley first learnt the lesson, the truth

of which he experienced afresh in every new crusade, that only if he shared in the sufferings of his fellows, could he hope to help them truly.

In March 1833 Ashley introduced his Bill, which restricted the labour of young persons between nine and eighteen years of age to ten hours per day and eight on Saturdays. There was to be no night work for those under twenty-one, and no children under nine were to be employed. Mill owners who failed to enforce the regulations were to be penalized on the third offence. The opposition was strong and well organized, for the industrialists had increased their representation in the reformed Parliament. The best of them were conscious that their factories provided better conditions than those obtaining under the old domestic system where the master had frequently been a bully and brute. They declared that Sadler's Committee had not dealt fairly with them. They demanded a new Commission, and in April this was granted by a majority of one.

On both sides of the Pennines there was an indignant outcry. Ashley, though bitterly disappointed, had laid down at the beginning that there was to be no violence and that only parliamentary methods were to be used. So he refrained from action while the Commission made its enquiry. The workers in the north were less docile. They passed angry resolutions expressing disgust at a visit "from an inquisitive itinerant, to enquire whether our children shall be worked more than ten hours a day; we are once and for all determined they shall not". At Leeds thousands of children paraded the streets, and at Bradford they mobbed the unfortunate Commissioners in the dinner-hour. These gentlemen, however, were not the sort to be unduly perturbed, and from the refuge of a mill yard took occasion to observe the real physical condition of the children. Happily they were men who would not be deflected in their search for truth by any terrorization either from above or below. Dr. Southwood Smith, the gentle physician to whom the fever-stricken streets of East London owed so much, and Edwin Chadwick, socialist, authoritarian, bureaucrat, visionary, all rolled into one dour Lancashire personality, had no doubt about their findings. The Commission made a preliminary statement that the children were not free agents, that their health was suffering and that therefore there was a case for legislation.

On the strength of this Ashley proceeded with his Bill. On June 17th it received its second reading without government opposition. When it reached the committee stage, however, Lord Althorp, the leader of the House, moved that the Bill should be referred to a select committee for redrafting on the lines suggested by the Commissioners, whose detailed recommendations were not yet published. By a majority of twenty-three Ashley defeated this proposal, but this was his last success. The Commissioners' report appeared next week and they recommended that the hours of work for children between nine and thirteen years of age should be still further reduced. They should only be employed for eight hours a day, but by using them in shifts the general output would not be affected. They did not advocate any protection for young persons between thirteen and eighteen. On July 18th Althorp moved that thirteen be substituted for eighteen in Ashley's Bill and carried his motion by 238 to 93. Cobbett commented cynically that the Commons had discovered that England's bulwark was not her Navy, nor the Bank, " but thirty thousand little girls ", for if they worked two hours a day less " our manufacturing superiority would depart from us ". Ashley declared that he surrendered the Bill into Althorp's hands, and he would only say, " Into whatever hands it passed, God prosper it." The Government Bill followed and in due course became the famous Factory Act of 1833. By the provisions of this Act no child under nine was to be employed, children between nine and thirteen were to work not more than the forty-eight-hour week with a maximum of nine hours a day, while " young persons " between thirteen and eighteen were to work not more than twelve hours a day as before. The hours were to be worked between 5.30 a.m. and 8.30 p.m., and the children were to attend school for at least two hours daily. Inspectors were appointed to see that the Act was duly enforced, and to this provision the success of the measure was largely due. Ashley freely recognized this, but he could not entirely rid himself of disappointment and chagrin for his personal failure. Southey wrote to him, "The Ministers would have done nothing unless you had forced them to it." But the north was still sullen. At the end of the session, the Ashleys and " Sir Babkins ", their son and heir, left England for a six months' foreign tour, and perhaps there were some in Lancashire and Yorkshire who shrugged their shoulders with the thought that, look at it how you may, Earl's son and factory worker belonged to a different world.

The position was not—it never is—as simple as it seems when regarded from the distance of a hundred years. Ashley's opponents were not monsters of iniquity. Sadler's Committee, owing mainly to his drive and determination, had put a body of facts before the House which could not be gainsaid. Members were in a quandary. How was their pride in England's expanding market, and their distrust, as good Benthamites, of any interference with trade, to be reconciled with their duty to the children? The compromise whereby the under-thirteens had their labour further reduced satisfied their consciences while any possible restriction of adult labour was avoided by the use of the shift system, and by leaving the hours of " young persons " uncontrolled. They were satisfied: not so the work-people of the north, whose ultimate aim was this very restriction of hours the gentlemen of Westminster disliked.

There were great stirrings in the north during these years between the passing of the Reform Bill and Victoria's accession. Disraeli has described them in the pages of *Sybil*, and his picture of Mowbray, with its Temple of the Muses and the pulsing life of the Saturday evening market, show that the squalor and misery of uncontrolled industrialism had its brighter side. Where there is youth and vigour, happiness, however fleeting and emaciated, will keep breaking through, and more than happiness: vision and hope. Robert Owen provided a rallying-point with his plans for a Grand National Consolidated Trade Union, in which scheme Fielden was his loyal supporter. But fear of ridicule, a certain mental laziness, and maybe the craftsman's preference for a definite job well done to vague plans for an uncertain future, have always made English folk suspicious of "Grand National" schemes. The energy and enthusiasm which Owen had stirred in his supporters turned to Chartism with its specific political demands.

Ashley regarded all such ebullition with distrust. He was conservative all through, and he may well have found his northern friends a little trying. He was beginning to feel his isolation. Since Wellington's eclipse, his party chief was the enigmatic Robert Peel, and the men had little use for each other. For a few brief months in 1834 Peel was in office, owing to a split among the Whigs over the Irish question. The new Prime Minister offered a minor post to Ashley, that of a Civil Commissioner in the Admiralty. It was a blow to the latter's pride; it showed him how his zeal in factory reform had ruined his chances of promotion. But Peel was only in power for a few months; after the elections the Whigs resumed office with Melbourne at their head, the poorer by the defection of Stanley and Graham, two of their bright young men.

Ashley saw his hopes and ambitions as a statesman fading into oblivion, but he barely had time to regret them. Much as the enthusiasts had disliked Althorp's Bill it had proved valuable, especially in the appointment of inspectors, thanks to the calibre of the men who were employed. So when a reactionary member in 1836 proposed an amending Bill lowering the age of control from thirteen to eleven, Ashley's aid was at once invoked to combat it. The Short Time Committees had been backing another champion, a Mr. Hindley, who advocated the restriction of motive power as the surest way of shortening hours, but when a parliamentary crisis arose he lacked both the skill and the standing which Ashley possessed. Owing to the latter's efforts the amending Bill was passed by two votes only, so slender a

majority that it was withdrawn. But so hard-won a success
did not give much hope for the Ten-Hour Bill that was still
the reformer's aim. Hindley in '36 and Ashley in '37 were
about to bring the measure forward, but both in turn withdrew with the consent of the Short Time Committees, so
obvious was it that opinion in the Commons was not yet ripe
for a further advance. These were difficult years. The ten-
hour movement was becoming merged in the Chartist agitation; Oastler was growing increasingly vituperative; Hindley
was in disrepute when his own firm was fined for a breach of
the Factory Act. Ashley himself had a jolt in '39 when Peel
was asked to form a government and insisted on the resignation of the Whig Ladies of the Bedchamber. He asked
Ashley to accept a post in the Royal Household. "Everything rushed before my mind; the trivialities of a court life,
the loss of time, the total surrender of my political occupation. . . ." Yet there could only be one answer for a Tory
asked to serve his Queen. Ashley replied that if Peel
thought he was the right man he would accept the office of
chief scullion. But after three glorious days Peel's second
tenure of office ended as suddenly as it had begun. Queen
Victoria had a will of her own and, as yet unschooled by
her gentle despot Albert, had no intention of changing the
Ladies of the Bedchamber. Another political crisis was over
and Melbourne's moribund Government had yet another
lease of life.

Ashley got on with his job of factory reform. So far all
that had been achieved applied only to the cotton mills.
But there were children suffering untold misery in the silk
and woollen factories, in the pin-making industry, in a
hundred other trades. True to his scientific bent of mind
that always demanded the facts, Ashley had been in the
north investigating for himself. Despite such setbacks as
Oastler's imprisonment for debt and the abortive Chartist
agitation, he concentrated on the one object of extending
factory control, and to this end in 1840 he urged the appointment of two Commissions of Enquiry, the one into the
working of the 1833 Act, the second into conditions in the

mines and other industries.   The fate of his motion was for
a while uncertain.   It was midnight and the House was
rapidly thinning.   But an unexpected division caused the
Government Whips to recall their members, and Ashley
seized the opportunity to move his motion in the small
hours, impressing even the most hardened members by his
fervent appeal.   "I have been bold enough to undertake
this task because I must regard the objects of it as being
created as ourselves by the same Maker, redeemed by the
same Saviour and destined to the same immortality."   And
yet in the pin industry, as he pointed out, children set to
work at the age of five and were worn out by fifteen, living
as best they could on "plunder, prostitution and pauperism".
"It is right," he concluded quietly, no hint of irony in his
voice, "that the country should know at what cost its pre-
eminence is purchased."   The country's representatives, for
very shame, agreed to his moderate request for full investigation, and upon the issue of a report next year the Government agreed to introduce bills amending the Factory Act
and extending its provisions to the lace industry.   But Melbourne fell from power in May 1841 and Ashley's hopes
were disappointed.   Good Tory that he was, he could not help
welcoming the change of government, but in his heart of
hearts he doubted whether Peel would be a better friend to
the children than the Whigs had proved.   For himself, the
change might mean a renewed opportunity of political influence, but during the summer as he visited the north and
met more closely the working men whose fortunes had
become so entangled with his own, he vowed that he would
accept office under no leader who would not support the
cause for which he stood.

III

Motive Power

IN a pen picture of Ashley written in 1838 he was described
as a man of tall and graceful figure and exceptional good
looks, with dark hair, deeply set blue eyes, well-chiselled
features, and a mouth small but firm, the whole giving an
impression of grace but also of determination. "To judge
from the set form of the lips you would say that he seldom
if ever acted from an impulse in his life. All that Lord
Ashley does seems to be done from conviction and principle, and not even a muscle dares to move without an order
from headquarters. Every separate lock of his hair appears
to curl because it has a reason for so doing and knows that
to be the right course of conduct."

It is not wholly an attractive portrait, not, at any rate, to
this age in which the rigid self-discipline of the Victorians
is at a discount. Undoubtedly the repressions of his childhood gave him a certain hypersensitiveness which twisted
out of the straight a nature already sufficiently intense.
Nor in this respect did his religion help him. The Evangelical tradition, with its stress on man's innate sinfulness
and its suspicion of many natural and healthy impulses,
deepened his reserve and made it more difficult for him to
throw off the moods of depression which frequently assailed
him. On the other hand his religion did give him that
personal approach to Christ which made him give help to
all in need. Here again the influences of his childhood
were apparent. His faith in Christ's nearness was founded
on the simple teaching of Maria Millis at a time when the
remoteness and coldness of his parents made personal
affection the most precious and necessary thing in his life.
Maria's own love for him made the things real she told
him about Jesus, whose redeeming power was symbolized
in the child's mind by her own comforting presence. In
the bitter years after her death he turned to the Bible which

she had taught him to read, and his religion remained linked with the conception of unselfish love—the thing he had found in Maria and missed so sorely in his parents. So it was that throughout his life it seemed sacrilege to him that any individual should be maltreated by man, be he lunatic, factory-child or chimney-sweep, since to God he was a son.

Thus his religion coloured his whole approach to life and sustained him in all that he tried to do. At the age of sixty he said to an audience of young men: "No man, depend upon it, can persist from the beginning of his life to the end of it in a course of generosity, in a course of virtue, in a course of piety, and in a course of prayer, unless he is drawing from the fountain of Our Lord Himself." He never neglected that fountain of living water, and was throughout his life a good Churchman as well as a good Christian. He had not in his religion, any more than in his politics or social work, much use for speculation or intellectual niceties. He had little mercy, and, alas, no Christian sense of brotherhood either for the " Puseyites ", whose love of ritual and the sacraments seemed to him a flirtation with Rome, or with the Christian Socialists whose love of humanity was equal to his own. In his youth he had also abhorred dissent, but as he worked with dissenters he came to realize how much they had in common in the service of the same Master. It was indeed a pity that he could not in similar fashion find common ground with the other branches of his own church. He never let his intense antagonism to the Oxford Movement colour with personal acrimony his letters to Dr. Pusey, his cousin and one-time friend, but he feared lest the preoccupation of the High Church clergy with sacerdotal tradition should blind them to their practical duties towards their fellow men. He forgot, in this respect, the power of God to guide the hearts that love Him, for it has not fallen out in the way he feared. The Anglo-Catholics of to-day have become in many parts of England leaders and fighters in the cause of social righteousness.

In 1840, however, it was still to the laymen of the
Evangelical persuasion that one looked for the drive and
the solid body of opinion which would make possible
advances in the moral welfare of ordinary people. And
since Ashley was regarded as their leader and his religion
was the basis of his whole way of life, one should not go
further without a passing glance at the meaning and
nature of the Evangelical movement. It was closely connected with Methodism, and had in the beginning, before
it was choked with respectability, something of the same
missionary fervour. At the end of the seventeenth century,
the immolation of the Non-jurors, saintly men denied the
opportunity of service, and the spiritual lethargy which
was the price the Latitudinarians had to pay for their immersion in party politics, cast a blight over the Anglican
communion, despite the quiet persistence of much personal devotion and the occasional appearance of such intellectual giants as Berkeley and Warburton. Such virtues as
the eighteenth-century Church possessed were like those of
the State, based on balance and good breeding and a distrust of emotion. Upon this calm exterior the influence of
Wesley broke resoundingly in the mid-years of the century,
shattering the Church's complacency as surely as the
citizen armies of France were to shatter the security of the
political *status quo*. His missionary zeal and practical
ability, the fervour of Whitfield and Charles Wesley's
hymns made Methodism a force that swept with increasing
strength through a country thirsty for a live religion.
When Methodism gradually organized itself as a separate
Church there remained in the Anglican body an Evangelical revival which owed much to Wesley and Whitfield.
In one important respect it differed from Methodism: the
Evangelicals remained sound, if uncritical, members of the
Church of England; they might not be specialists in theo-
logical subtleties but they loved the practices and respected
the discipline of the Anglican Communion, and their life
as Christians was centred in the Parish Church. With
Wesley's idea of itinerant preachers they had little

C

sympathy. The daily example of the Parish Priest's life and character no less than his Sunday sermon was their guide and inspiration, and in the fellowship of the re-invigorated parish Anglicans again savoured that sense of comradeship and united effort in the cause of Christ which the Dissenters had long experienced. Such a congregation was that which sat under the Rev. John Venn at Clapham, called in friendly derision the "Clapham sect". Its members were well-to-do: the Thorntons, rich London merchants, who under the impulse of religion spent most of their fortune on charity; Zachary Macaulay, the serious father of a brilliant son; Lord Dartmouth, "a peer who wears a coronet and prays"; and Pitt's friend Wilberforce, the gifted, charming, eager young man who might have done anything with his life and chose to do good.

It was in their absorption in movements for the betterment of mankind, their actions firmly based on their belief in Christ as the centre of their faith and their living, that they enriched the Anglican tradition, rather than by any new philosophy or interpretation of dogma. It was this kind of religion, with its dual concept of love of God and duty to Man, which the young Anthony had imbibed at the knees of Maria Millis. In the passing of forty years it may have deepened in quality, but it had not changed its nature. To the end he remained, in his limitations as well as in his powers, "an Evangelical of Evangelicals".

No wonder that he stood a little apart in the society to which he belonged by virtue of his birth and breeding. Yet he was at home there, as he was in the back streets and crowded tenements he was just beginning to explore. He visited Windsor and dined with the Queen. "She is so kind and good to me and mine," he reflected. "Poor soul, she was low-spirited. I do deeply feel for her; 'uneasy lies the head that wears a crown'. Oh, that she knew what alone makes a yoke easy and a burden light." Perhaps the young Queen, preoccupied with her own thoughts about the horridness of Peel and her longing for dear Melbourne, who always made her feel comfortable without telling her what to do, found her quiet guest, so austerely handsome, so uncompromisingly good, a trifle overwhelming. It was well for Ashley that just now, when the vastness of the tasks he had undertaken deepened his natural severity, a humanizing influence entered his life in the form of a most unexpected friendship.

On December 16th, 1839, he entered in his diary: "This day my mother-in-law will be married to Palmerston." It did not seem an event likely to affect him closely. But slowly during the succeeding decade the acquaintanceship of Ashley and Palmerston ripened into intimacy, the more valuable to both because of the diversity of their nature. "Pam" was fifty-five years old, and as devoid of staunch orthodox religious roots as Ashley was the reverse: he was shrewd, worldly, unreliable, socially approachable, all things to all men, everything that Ashley was not. But they had this in common: an unquenchable interest in facts and a liking for the common man. Their freedom from convention and an inbred conviction of their own superiority enabled them to strike out on lines of their own, whether it was championing the chimney-boys or flaunting British prestige in the face of Europe.

In 1839 Palmerston "walked by himself" among the Whigs, much in the same way that Ashley did among the Tories. Originally one of Canning's bright young men, he had taken less easily to the guise of Whiggism than the indolent Melbourne. But he enjoyed his work at the Foreign Office, where his liking for independent action had angered the Queen and perturbed the Government. Through thick and thin he retained the loyalty and affection of Lady Cowper, his childhood's friend. When she became a widow they were married, and the gay and charming society hostess at whose house you met everyone and where everyone felt at home proved a loyal and valuable helpmeet to her husband. She well deserved the title "the best of Whigs and always the soundest of Palmerstonians".[1]

Lady Palmerston had always been a good friend to Ashley,

[1] Guedalla: *Palmerston*, p. 227.

whom she now introduced to her husband. Their first subject of mutual interest was Palestine, in whose future each was equally concerned, the Foreign Minister with an eye on Turkey, the Evangelical dreaming of a Holy Land recovered for the Christian Faith. After discussing the politics, economics and finance of the Near East, Pam was forced to advance to religion, which he found a new and fascinating subject. Both men grew at an early stage of their acquaintanceship to respect the other, and with the passing of years this respect and liking deepened into real affection. It was thus with a lighter heart than usual that Ashley entered upon his fortieth year, serene in mind, vigorous in body and exceptionally happy in his family life and his growing children. A successful visit to Scotland and the north of England in the autumn of 1839 had culminated in a renewal of friendly relations with his father. The Earl was getting on in years—perhaps some mutual friend put in a kindly word—perhaps the Palmerston marriage made him regard his son's circle as worth knowing. Anyhow, there were friendly approaches and Ashley spent more than one Christmas at St. Giles with his father. "The church was alive with holly," he wrote one Christmas Day, "and thronged by a decent, well-behaved, well-dressed congregation. The sacrament was administered to about a hundred communicants . . . of whom I and my father formed a part, reconciled, God be praised, and made one again after so large an interval of human life." And afterwards, in a bout of sunny weather, he worked in the garden cutting down bushes and quoting to himself, "God first planted a garden." "This is the thing I have ever desired and now I have my own way."

It was a time of quiet content, occasioned by the simple and satisfying things which money and fame cannot buy. Of such is the stuff of happiness, the by-product of a life of unselfish service.

IV

Down the Mines

IN 1841 Robert Peel and Lord John Russell faced each other across the floor of the House; Peel, who understood so much about so many things and so little about himself that he continued until the end of his life to think himself a Tory, and Russell, " thin-lipped and earnest, a small embodiment of Whiggery ". A deeply religious man, full of charm and vivacity in his own family circle, but unable to get on easy terms with his inferiors, Russell appeared to take politics with an easy nonchalance, stealing away to the opera when a Cabinet tangle seemed insoluble. But once he was really roused, the small delicate figure seemed to be infused with a borrowed strength. It was worth bolting one's dinner and hurrying to Westminster ". . . when the steam is on, and languid Johnny glows to glorious John". Being a true Russell he was conscientious to a degree equalled only by Ashley, but because he was a Russell he was more interested in questions of constitutional law and civil liberty than in social and philanthropic measures. To Ashley he seemed to miss his opportunities of doing good. There was no sympathy between the two men, though at bottom they had more in common than Ashley had with Peel, his own party chief. But Peel and Russell alike failed to approach the manifold problems of 1830 to 1850 from Ashley's point of view.

The last years of Whig rule had been singularly barren, owing to Melbourne's paralysing leadership, but in 1841 Peel's accession to power made progress possible again. Peel had a much clearer conception than the Whigs of the economic difficulties that were strangling the country's life. The best way to solve the problem of the poor was to improve trade and increase prosperity all round. He was a difficult leader. When he was young, his father sent him to Harrow to learn to mix with others, but a boy's nature is not changed even by sending him to a good public school. Peel remained a solitary. Ashley sat next to him at dinner once, and described it as being in the "neighbourhood of an iceberg with a slight flaw on the surface". But the greater part of an iceberg is submerged, and beneath the cold exterior there was conviction and courage sufficient to make Peel a great man and to win him in time the love and respect of his Queen and of the people. He had something in him of eighteenth-century restraint. Ashley summed him up later as a man with "an abundance of human honesty and not much of divine faith; he will never do a dishonourable thing: he will be ashamed of doing a religious one".

Upon Peel's appointment as Prime Minister Ashley thought it his duty to write him a long letter advocating a strictly protestant attitude in religious matters. The letter must have strengthened Peel in his conviction that as a colleague Ashley would be utterly impossible. He did not invite him to join his government and, as once before, tactlessly offered him a subordinate place in the Royal Household.

Ashley was indignant. It seemed to him "a plain, cruel, unnecessary insult". The blow was the more bitter because for months Ashley had been steeling himself to say "No" if offered a high government post. He had been returned for Dorset in the general election, satisfying his farmers with the assertion that the cry for free corn was "both absurd and wicked". He had then gone to the north and identified himself yet more closely with the ten-hour agitation. The employers had made no bones about their intention of opposing any Bill he might introduce in the new session, and he realized that, in view of their attitude, he could not count on Peel's support. Hence his decision to refuse office, the final regretful surrender of the political ambition that had died so hard; hence the bitter feeling when denied even the luxury of saying "No".

That Christmas of 1841 was less happy than recent ones, for his wife was ill at her mother's home, and Ashley had to go to St. Giles alone to be with the children there. Without her, it was hard to find the peace and spiritual joy which the Christmas communion should have brought him, or to shut out the " turmoils and anxieties of the world ". In the New Year he wrote to Peel asking definitely what his attitude would be to " the further limitation of the hours of labour between the ages of thirteen and twenty-one ". To his letter he received an equally definite reply that Peel was not prepared to pledge himself or other members of the Government.

Seldom before or after did Ashley feel more isolated. " I feel sadly alone, I am like a pelican in the wilderness, or a sparrow on the housetops, I have no one with whom I can take counsel, no one to aid me, no one to cheer me." " They feel I am in the right and Peel in the Treasury," he declared as he looked round upon the new House of Commons. He wrote to the Short Time Committees urging them to persevere, and in March he was reconciled to Peel, shaking hands with him and avoiding all explanations. But in April he recorded, " People are already beginning to say, ' You will do nothing this year with your Factory Bill, the Government will have no time . . .' Meanwhile wrong, oppression, mutilation, death, with all the grim roll of physical and moral evils, are in full liberty."

Then in May the atmosphere was completely changed. After two years the Royal Commission[1] published its report on labour conditions in the mines. The House was shocked into amazed and pitying attention. No one had suspected the truth or had bothered to find it out. In our own day it needed the practical experience of " evacuees " driven from the towns by the overwhelming catastrophe of war, to bring home to many kindly English folk how the other half of England really lived. So it was a hundred years ago. The factual nature of the Mines report, its very restraint added to its effectiveness. It set itself to find answers to fourteen questions about the age, sex, and number of children working in the mines, the method of hire, their wages and the

[1] See above, p. 29.

nature of their employment, the hours worked and the provision of time for meals and holidays, the extent of night work, the numbers of accidents and the general treatment of the children and the effect upon their physical condition. Nothing could be more reasonable. But the result was startling. Seven was the usual age at which hard labour began for these poor scraps of humanity. "I say, Jonas . . . we have none under ten or eleven working in this mine," said one manager, and was unseasonably interrupted by a collier: "Sir, my boy is only a little more than four."

The main job of these youngsters was to take the place of beasts of burden when the galleries were too low for ponies to go easily along them. By means of chains fastened between their legs they dragged the trucks of coal along the dark, damp passages. "There are very few under six or seven who do it," said one apologetic mine's doctor. Some of the babes did have an easier, if mentally a more unnerving job, for they sat alone in the dark all day, opening and shutting the trap-doors for the wagons to pass through. The ventilation and safety of the mines depended on their doing this promptly, yet they were not even given a light. " I'm scared," said Sarah Gooder, aged eight. " I go at four and sometimes half-past three in the morning, and come out at five or half-past [in the afternoon]. Sometimes I sing when I've a light, but not in the dark, I dare not sing then." It was perhaps as well that complete ignorance and malnutrition kept them so little above the level of animals that evil imaginings may have tortured only a few of these young " trappers " as they waited in the blackness. To realize how degrading their general conditions were, the tyranny of the truck-shop and the brutality of the " buttees ", one must turn again to the pages of *Sybil* and shudder to think at what a cost England has made herself rich.

At Westminster they were particularly shocked to hear that girls in slacks worked alongside the boys, and Victorian respectability had some cause to be perturbed at the picture the report disclosed of adolescent girls in torn breeches working for men who were often naked, and losing all sense of natural restraint. "I have had many a twopence given me by the boatmen in the canal to show my breeches," one witness declared proudly. The collier and his girl "hurrier" often worked apart on lonely seams and sexual intercourse frequently took place. It might have been still more usual but for the deadening effect of habit. But few could escape being brutalized, and even those who married in due course and set up homes knew next to nothing of home-making and often worked underground for months after they had become pregnant. Babies were sometimes born down the mine, and within a fortnight the mother would be back at work again. Small wonder if many of the infants were still-born, while above ground "the bairns are much neglected while both parents work below, for neighbours, if they keep the children, they require as much as women sometimes earn, and neglect them."

To such a man as Ashley, there could be but one remedy: the exclusion of girls and women from the mines. The women, fearing that the enquiry would lead to this declared that they liked the work, while the men protested against the indecency of the Commissioners examining the girls in their working attire! The path of the reformer is not easy. But the colliers on the whole were agreed that the employment of women was a "shameful practice". "They are best out of pits, are lasses," said one. "I don't think nought about it. I am sure of it," said another.

The report unfolded itself page after page with fresh revelations of horror on every line. The young "hurriers" suffered intensely from headaches, for they had to use their heads to push their way through the passages sometimes not more than a yard high, and though they wore skull-caps to protect their hair they frequently went bald. They often worked for fourteen hours a day, with a certain amount of night work, no regular hours for meals, and hectic holidays immediately after pay-day and during the Wakes. There was no consistent ill-usage of the children, but they suffered as their elders did at the hands of the "buttees" (middle-men), who were often drunk with power which in their own small sphere was practically unlimited. The ordinary working man was as kindly then as now, and one lad's evidence was probably typical of many. "The men did not thump me very often. I was not very bad, only middling. I sometimes deserved it because I would not do as they told me."

The last section of the report dealt fully with the evil effects of physical strain and continuous overwork. Too tired to play or even to go to bed, the children would throw themselves on the hearthrug like dogs as soon as they entered their homes; the few who went to evening school were of course too tired to learn. Their growth was stunted, while the abnormal development of certain muscles gave them an air of deformity, and they frequently suffered from lung complaints and irritation of the skin. In fact, they were living lives unfit for animals, let alone human beings.

These were the facts that at Ashley's instigation had been gathered together and were now laid before the House. In June 1842 he introduced a Bill to exclude from the mines all women and girls and all boys under thirteen. For Ashley it was a great occasion. He had suffered his usual agony of doubt beforehand. Peel had given him a day for his Bill, but a lengthy debate on a question of privilege prevented him bringing it forward. "Never did I pass such an evening; expecting for six hours without food or drink to be called on at any moment." Before his next chance came the House was adjourned for a week owing to an attempted assassination of the Queen. When it reassembled Ashley postponed his Bill yet again so that the Prime Minister could deal with some urgent business. But he was getting rattled. "These repeated delays have tired my patience and stumbled my faith," he wrote, "God forgive me." But at length, on June 7th, he introduced his Bill. "Only be strong and of a good courage," God's words to Joshua came into his mind as he awaited the ordeal, and his nervousness vanished. He excelled himself in the ensuing speech. "The success has been wonderful, yes, really wonderful—for two hours the House listened so attentively that you might have heard a pin drop. . . . Even Joseph Hume was touched." Cobden rushed impulsively across the House to shake Ashley by the hand, and Ashley was as joyous as previously he had been depressed. "You may this night," he told the members, "by a cheap and harmless vote, invigorate the hearts of thousands of your country people, enable them to walk erect in newness of life to enter on the enjoyment of their inherited freedom, and avail themselves (if they will accept them) of the opportunities of virtue and morality and religion." When Parliament responded he wrote in his Diary, "It has given me hopes for the Empire; hopes for its permanence; hopes for its service in the purposes of the Messiah!"

The Bill left the Commons practically unaltered, but in the Upper House it was challenged by the coal-owning interests headed by Lord Londonderry, who drew reassuring pictures of the young trappers, amusing themselves by sharpening sticks and chalking pictures on the wall, and uttered the usual derogatory remarks about education to which die-hards are prone in every generation. The Bill got through, but it was considerably amended; the age at which boys could be employed for instance was reduced to ten. In order to save the measure, the amendments were accepted, but Ashley wrote of the peers: "Never have I seen such a display of selfishness, frigidity to every human sentiment, such ready and happy self-delusion." He prayed earnestly that the day might be long delayed when he should join their number and put an end to his own "public usefulness".

The Mines Bill became law: in some ways it was Ashley's greatest legislative triumph. It had one unfortunate result; it threw out of work in the "hungry forties" a number of women who were on the verge of starvation and unlikely to appreciate Ashley's efforts on their behalf! But such unhappy readjustments cannot nullify the value of a measure which put an end to much human misery, and extended yet further the principle that no community has the right to obtain for itself comfort and material prosperity at the cost of prostituting its weaker and less fortunate members.

For Ashley himself, the Mines Act was but one step forward along a road whose end was still out of sight. The Ten-Hour Bill with all that it implied had still to be fought out at Westminster. There were scores of industries in which young people were still unprotected. In addition he was becoming steadily more convinced that restrictive legislation in itself was not enough. The aim of all who worked for God's kingdom must be the creation of a generation of children practising the Christian virtues and well-grounded in the Christian faith. On February 28th, 1843, he made the greatest speech of his career when he moved an address to the Queen " to take into her instant and serious consideration the best means of diffusing the benefits and blessings of a moral and religious education among the working classes of her people ". " We owe to the poor of our land a weighty debt," he declared. " We call them improvident and immoral and many of them are so, but that improvidence and that immorality are the results in a great measure of our neglect, and not a little of our example. We owe them too the debt of kinder language and more frequent intercourse. . . ." Those words mark the beginning of a new line of thought which was eventually to moderate Ashley's own career and to divide him from his north-country friends. It was not enough to work for the oppressed at Westminster. If indeed " a virtuous, wise and understanding people " were to emerge from " the mighty multitude of feeble bodies and untaught minds " that constituted " the masses ", men like himself must go out into their midst and learn to help and teach and understand.

V

"Twelve Hours or Ten?"

THEY were lean and hungry days in 1843; England was well in the trough of a trade cycle, and while the mill-owners clamoured for the repeal of the Corn Laws and inveighed against the miserable conditions of country life, the land-owners retaliated by demanding factory reform and backed up the workers in their cry for a ten-hour day. Politicians and theorists, with no guidance from precedents, aligned themselves with little regard to party loyalties, so that among the Whigs, Palmerston and Russell were on one side, Melbourne and Bright on the other, and only the firm hand of Peel kept the Tories in a semblance of unity. The Free-Traders distrusted all control, and the phrase "ten-hour day" had much the same effect on them as "common ownership" might have to-day. Part of Peel's opposition to the movement came from his hope that if he conciliated the mill-owners on this point they would not force his hand in the matter of corn-law repeal. But to Ashley the Ten-Hour Bill was the necessary precursor of all further reform, and part of a greater issue, the gradual emergence of a self-respecting working class.

It was as a further step in this direction that he stressed the importance of education. The immediate result of his February speech was the introduction of a Government Bill, sponsored by Graham, the one-time Whig, to establish a measure of schooling in the factories. The education clauses in the 1833 Act had been shamelessly evaded. An old dame from the neighbouring village, a caretaker who could not write his own name, any old man who could be found, kept the children quiet for the two hours a day specified by law, and taught them, sometimes in the coal-hole, what little they knew themselves of the A.B.C. Graham was a Scot and therefore intelligent about educa-

tion. He suggested that a committee of which the Vicar
and churchwardens were to be members should undertake
the task of making the factory schools efficient and satisfactory.

But he had counted without the Nonconformist conscience! His Bill raised an outcry that no attempt at compromise on his part could quell. He laid down that there
should be no doctrinal teaching. Ashley was perturbed
for he distrusted grammar and syntax without definite
Christian instruction to ensure that the pupil made good
use of his knowledge, but rather than see the Bill collapse
he accepted Graham's proposal, trusting that the spread of
learning would at least secure a wider use of the Bible. But
the Free Churchmen were still suspicious; thousands of
petitions reached Graham and he eventually withdrew the
Bill. Ashley sorrowfully realized that an agreed syllabus
was still an impossibility and he pinned his faith for the
future to the Church schools. England has paid a great
price for the unhappy divisions of Christians in her midst,
and only those who have traced out the embittered dis-
putes of the nineteenth century can appreciate to the full
the glorious opportunity of to-day.

In February 1844 Graham introduced the new Government Bill for factory reform. The educational clauses had
been dropped and the issue of the length of working hours
was squarely faced in a measure which prohibited night
work for young persons under eighteen and laid down that
all women, whatever their age, should be included as
" young persons " and, like them, should work not more
than twelve hours a day.

And now the battle was joined. The Short Time Committees were convinced that unless the fundamental of the
ten-hour day were established, giving to the workers time
to get away for a period from the soul-deadening noise of
the machines, all other benefits of the factory laws, all
schemes for educational or sanitary reform would remain
an empty mockery. They sent delegates to London to
canvas leading statesmen; by every means of propaganda

they possessed they were out to make the issue clear. Two of them called upon Lord Palmerston. He received them with his usual urbanity, but suggested that since nowadays machines did all the work, the hardship to the children must have been exaggerated. The two north-country men looked round the spacious dining-room where they had been received. They asked his lordship's permission to stage a practical demonstration. Barely giving him time to reply, they began to move the furniture about. Palmerston, interested, called in the footman to assist. They piled the chairs in the middle of the room to represent the spinning-mule, and the future Prime Minister—and his footman—were asked to enact the part of the children, and were shown how they would have to walk to and fro in tending the machine. Lady Palmerston was waiting upstairs to go out. Puzzled by the delay, she came down to see what had occurred. She found her husband walking here and there across the dining-room followed by the footman. Fortunately she was an understanding wife and Palmerston was an honest man. He agreed, as he thankfully paused for breath, that the children might easily walk twenty miles a day. Once converted he proved a staunch supporter of the cause.

The first critical debate took place on March 15th when the Bill had reached the committee stage. The second clause prohibited the employment of protected persons between 8 p.m. and 6 a.m.; Ashley moved an amendment that 6 p.m. be substituted for 8 p.m., thus in effect shortening the working day by two hours and bringing the principle of "twelve hours or ten" for the first time directly under discussion. The debate lasted into the small hours, and Ashley spoke for two and a half hours, pleading for a little leisure for the workers, "a time to live and a time to die, a time for those comforts that sweeten life, and a time for those duties that abound". Graham followed immediately to announce the Government's decided opposition to his motion, and John Bright followed with a personal attack on Ashley, declaring that he looked at Lancashire through a telescope, but used the wrong end of the glass when he turned it upon St. Giles and the wretched conditions of the Dorset villages. At two in the morning, with tempers exacerbated and nothing achieved, the debate was adjourned.

Ashley spent an uneasy week-end. He was worried about St. Giles and had recently suggested an investigation of conditions in Dorset, which had not only disturbed his constituents but had led to a new breach with his father. But he could not talk about family quarrels to John Bright.

On Sunday he received various unofficial communications from the Government, urging him not to press his motion. But this roused the fighting spirit in him. On Tuesday, March 19th, the debate was resumed in an atmosphere of intense excitement. Peel threw down the gauge. He instanced the numerous other industries in which there was no control. Was the House prepared to legislate for all of these? Much to his discomfiture, there was a cheer and a determined cry of " Yes! " " Even for Agriculture? " Again, " Yes! " Peel sat down with the curt statement, " I cannot and I will not acquiesce in the proposal of the noble Lord."

Russell, a convert like Palmerston to the ten-hour cause, followed with an able, reasoned speech, in which, mindful of his attitude when the Whigs had been in power, he forgave himself for his own inconsistency. At length, the House divided; Ashley's amendment was carried by nine votes (179 to 170) and the principle of the shorter day accepted for the first time by the House of Commons. Graham rose to his feet. He declared that he had an " insuperable objection " to this decision. The House would have a chance to reconsider it when they reached the eighth clause which was directly concerned with the length of the working day. With this parting shot, he moved the adjournment.

Graham was a man of administrative ability but narrow sympathy, with an imperious streak in him which made him loath to accept defeat. He was a self-opinionated man. He annoyed people by cocking his hat on the wrong side of the head, or leaning back in his seat in the Commons " with his head thrown back and his eyes fixed on the windows over the gallery as if there was nothing going on in the House worth his listening to ". He meant the Bill to be his Bill and not Ashley's, and agreed with Greville's dictum, " We are just now over-run with philanthropy and God knows where it will stop." Ashley, conscious of this implacable hostility, felt little jubilation, though he knew much had been accomplished; " struggle as they will the question is passed; it may be delayed in its final accomplishment, but surely it cannot be reversed. God give us faith, faith, faith! "

The eighth clause was reached on Friday, March 22nd. This stated the length of hours to be worked by young persons. Two divisions were taken, the first on the Government motion that twelve should be the number inserted; the second on Ashley's motion that it should be ten. In the first case, the Government were defeated by 186 votes to 183; in the second case, twelve hours having been rejected, the House also said " No " to ten hours, and Ashley also was defeated by 188 to 181. Five members voted " No " on each occasion. In such strange ways, at times, does democracy work in England.

What would happen next? Most people expected the Government to suggest eleven hours as a compromise, but on Monday, 25th, Graham stated that the Bill was in such a muddle that the Government would introduce a new one and still stand by the twelve-hour clause. He derided these new-fangled ideas as " Jack Cade legislation ", and Ashley interrupted angrily, " Let me ask the House what was it gave birth to Jack Cade." This was the mood in which the House adjourned for the Easter recess.

Graham introduced the new Bill on May 3rd, and Ashley gave notice of his intention to move the clause reducing the hours from twelve to ten at a later stage. He described it as a night of trouble. " They fired at me without mercy and left me, like a portrait of St. Sebastian, shot through and through by their arrows. . . . Strong in my cause and conduct, weak in my capacity." But when a few days later the third reading was reached and he moved his clause, he spoke with his old verve and conviction and stirred the House to fresh enthusiasm as he described his hopes for "renewed understanding between master and man", and declared that "amidst much injustice, and somewhat of calumny, we have at last lighted such a candle in England as by God's blessing shall never be put out".

The House adjourned at 1 a.m., and when the debate was resumed after the week-end it was in a very different atmosphere. Heroics were all very well, but Peel settled matters, once for all, by making the division a vote of censure on the Government, and stating that he would retire if defeated. In such a predicament loyal party men had no real choice. Ashley's amendment was lost by a majority of 138, "utterly, singularly, prodigiously defeated".

Except for some fire-works from Brougham in the Lords, nothing further occurred to impede the passing of the Bill. It became law on June 6th, and despite its shortcomings did much to improve the conditions of the workers, reducing the hours for "under-thirteens" and making some useful regulations about the use of machinery. The Short Time Committees drew what comfort they could from the fact that the principle for which they were fighting had been accepted by the House in its vote of March 19th. The majority still looked to Ashley as their leader and guide at Westminster, but some already contrasted his Fabian methods with the fire and directness of Lord John Manners, who boldly advocated new remedies for the evils of a new age. The Government themselves wondered if Ashley might be won over, and made him a tentative offer of the lord-lieutenancy of Ireland. The difficulties and possibilities of the job fascinated him, but there was only one honest reply. He could accept nothing which would limit his chances of fighting for the ten-hour day. He might do it

in his own way and it might not always be the way of
Oastler and Stephens and the rest, but for him as for them
it was little short of a religion, this faith in the fairer world
that would come when men had time to live as well as to
work.

VI

The Sick in Mind

A CRITIC once asserted that Ashley was no statesman. " If I were," he retorted, " I should not be such a fool as to attack every interest and one half of mankind." To tell in one chapter of his efforts for the factory children, in the next of his work for the insane, in a third of his interest in ragged schools, is the only way to retain a modicum of clarity; but this was not his life. His life was a crowded, richly coloured affair in which chimney-sweeps and the cottages at St. Giles, lace-makers and pickpockets and the Queen at Windsor, matins on Sunday and his little boys' upbringing, Westminster and the Short Time Committees, all claimed his attention, and he gave of himself freely to them all. No ordered chapters can give any impression of the complexity, the seething humanity, the breathlessness of his days, in which every minute was filled three times over, and yet somehow time was always found to help anyone in distress. " I was an hungred and ye gave me meat; thirsty and ye gave me drink." How could anyone dare ever to say " No "?

The years 1844 and 1845 illustrate better than most the complexity of his parliamentary activities. The ten-hour day had not yet been achieved, thousands of children in other than textile industries were still unprotected. And now the lunacy laws were in urgent need of revision. Moreover, in an age when the scope of legislation was extending, the preliminary enquiry and the follow-through were important parts of the business, and public service on boards and commissions took up a considerable amount of Ashley's time and suited his type of genius. For it was always by a patient accumulation of facts, by finding out the truth and by insisting upon subsequent action, that he achieved so much, rather than by blazing a new trail or by initiating startling reforms, and his sense of personal responsibility for the evils he was combating made him ready and willing to take any amount of trouble over individual cases.

In his work for the insane all these characteristics appear; the years of faithful service on the Lunacy Commission; the patient and often painful investigation of special cases; and the insistent hammering of the facts into the hard heads of his colleagues at Westminster. He had long been conscious of the problem of the sick in mind. Since the middle of the previous century, Justices had the power of locking up any dangerous lunatic, and in the absence of sufficient or suitable asylums this power had been grossly abused. It was still felt to be something of a disgrace to have a " madman " in the family, and anyone of means who showed odd proclivities might be spirited away into a private " madhouse " and never be heard of again. In most counties there was no refuge for the poor lunatic except the workhouse, where he was fortunate if he were left in peace to a crabbed existence, chained to a piece of furniture or in the corner of a solitary outhouse. The old medieval idea that the devil himself had taken possession of the insane was the dark side of that other kindly fancy that an angel kept a friendly eye on the vagaries of the village idiot. So it was not un-common for a lunatic to be plunged in cold water or be subjected to various petty torments—and some not so petty —on the pretence that the evil spirit was being exorcised. Those sadistic impulses, from which few men are entirely immune, brought hundreds of Londoners, respectable people in the estimation of their neighbours, on an outing to Bedlam, where they cheerfully paid twopence for a sight of the raving lunatics behind iron bars.

As usual improvement came by degrees. In 1774 Commis-sioners who were also medical men were appointed to inspect all houses where more than one insane person was confined, but since this measure did not apply to public asylums, and no punitive powers were invested in the Commissioners, the good they could do was infinitesimal. In 1793 the Society of Friends founded a Retreat in York where humane and quiet care and attention produced remarkable results. At the same time in Paris, Dr. Pinel was also experimenting in the effects of kindliness, and just as fifty years later the Quaker Lister and the French Catholic Pasteur were by their joint efforts to do so much to overthrow the tyranny of bodily pain, so now the French doctor and the English Quietists opened a gate of deliverance for the mentally afflicted.

One of the brighter sides of Perceval's reactionary Government was the activity of George Rose, Vice-President of the Board of Trade, who exposed the iniquitous state of things existing in many public asylums. Efforts were made to amend the laws, but the progressives in the House of Lords could make no headway against peers who seemed to regard the desire to inspect and control asylums as an insidious attack on property. It was not till 1828 that Robert Gordon, seconded by Ashley, introduced the motion that resulted in two new laws being passed, the one empowering Justices to order the building of asylums, and the other appointing fifteen Commissioners (instead of the previous five) with wider powers of control and supervision, not as yet over Bedlam, but over all other madhouses in London and within seven miles around. Five of these Commissioners were still to be medical men and were to receive a salary for their services, ten were to be unpaid, another example of the voluntary system so deeply rooted in English life whereby time and energy unstinted have been given by so many in the public service. Ashley became a Commissioner at once and Chairman in 1834, and to the end of his life continued the onerous and nerve-wracking work of visiting asylums, interviewing patients, dealing with licences and accumulating facts, the munitions necessary for the next advance.

The next thing done, in 1842, was to extend the principle of supervision to the provinces. Commissioners were appointed to investigate conditions outside London, where obviously there was urgent need of reform. When Ashley introduced this measure (sandwiched between the Mines Act, efforts in the cause of Public Health, and violent correspondence on the subject of the Oxford Chair of Poetry) some criticized him for not being radical enough. But he was not a Radical, and it was his usual method of procedure, and the report of this Commission in 1844 gave him the information which enabled him next year to introduce successfully the Bill which has been called the "Magna Carta" of the Insane. By this Act all asylums, except Bedlam, were placed under the control of the Commissioners. (At Bedlam vested interest was sufficiently strong to exclude it from the national scheme for another eight years.) The Lunacy Commission now became a permanent body with increased powers, and Ashley introduced a supplementary Bill making it obligatory for all counties to provide suitable asylums so that at long last adequate accommodation was in sight. In addition the provision of case-books and regular medical attendance suggested the possibilities of curative treatment.

The most difficult problem was how to prevent improper detention when the mental state was still uncertain. Stringent regulations were laid down; in the case of a pauper, in addition to a doctor, a Poor Law official or magistrate had also to see the patient; in other cases, the certificates of two medical men were required. Yet the public was not satisfied, and the work of the Commission was punctuated during the next forty years by incidents and newspaper agitations regarding alleged abuses. These gradually crystallized into a demand for the addition of a magistrate's signature to that of the medical men. Shaftesbury in his old age resisted this demand, mainly because he feared that this alteration (which did in fact become law after his death) might lessen the chances of mental cases being placed under proper supervision while there was still the possibility of a cure.

There were a host of minor enactments in the measures of 1845 which helped to ameliorate the wretched lot of the sick in mind. Rules for holidays, the extension of visiting hours, provision of proper food, in all these small ways their life was made more bearable as the result of Ashley's patient observation as he went from one asylum to another, "jump-

ing for joy " when he noted improvements and asking himself, " Do we go fast enough? "

The success in passing the Lunacy Bills was Ashley's great
achievement in 1845. He had the support of the Government, and to his pleased surprise Graham himself seconded
the motion to introduce them in a " very kind and fervid
speech ". Relations between the two men had again been
strained that spring owing to Ashley's efforts on behalf of
the children in the Calico Print Works. He had been intensely distressed to find that the length of their day
frequently extended to eighteen hours under conditions
extremely injurious to health and particularly to their eyesight. The thought of these small sufferers clouded all his
spring. A lovely morning evoked from him the cry, " Let
everything that has breath, Praise the Lord. Aye, children
in Print works, no less than birds and beasts and creeping
things." "We are desperately wicked, we who do such
things and we who do not prevent them," he had written
earlier. He introduced a Bill to protect them, but the
novelty of factory reform had worn off in the Commons, and
the cool and subtly hostile Graham again spiked Ashley's
guns by offering to support the measure, but only when
modified as he desired. Instead of an eight-hour day for
all children under thirteen, Ashley had to be content with
the abolition of night work, the exclusion of children under
eight, and a modicum of education for the others. He had
again to choose between accepting the little the Government would give, or demanding more and ruining the
chances of the Bill. As usual he took what he could get,
and began again.

It was on June 6th, the very day that he moved for leave
to introduce the Lunacy Bills and Graham promised the
Government's support, that the Calico Print Works Bill was
accepted in the Lords. For once he was jubilant. The twin
success on the same day wiped out the memory of the hot
weary summer and the incompleteness of the Print Works
Bill. For once he was conscious of friendly sympathy, not
isolation, as he looked round the House.

It was indeed a time of great achievement. Since the Tories took office he had dealt in turn with the Mines, the Factory Bill of '44, the Calico Print Bill, and the Insane. It was a great account on the credit side. There remained on the debit side the unsettled question of the ten-hour day, and the other children! He could not rest till they were all safe—the waifs in the London streets, the child-labourers in other industries, the little climbing boys.

His hands were more than full. Happily during these strenuous years he enjoyed the sustaining background of an idyllic family life. The Palmerstons made them welcome at their country home in the holidays, but the old house in Brook Street, Grosvenor Square, was their usual headquarters. Ashley's heart was in his work in London, and his conscience never let him rest happy for long away from the crowded streets.

They were always short of money. Anthony, their eldest son, was at a preparatory school in the Isle of Wight. In the summer of '44 they had promised the three younger boys to take them across to the island to bring their brother home. But the trip was not accomplished without some heart-searchings in the Diary. " Very expensive, but we had incautiously made the promise." And so to the island they went, Francis, Maurice and Evelyn; somehow or other the outing was financed and a precious memory of July sunshine was garnered for the darker days ahead.

Not long afterwards Anthony went to Rugby. Eton had been considered, but his father thought it too near to Windsor. He had his own views on the question of public schools. " We must have nobler, deeper, sterner stuff," he wrote, " less of refinement and more of truth, more of the inward, not so much of the outward gentleman." He wanted his son not to be afraid of being laughed at, and to remember that it was a serious responsibility to have wealth and influence and not just an opportunity to show off. Above all he wished him to abide by his baptismal promise, to continue Christ's faithful soldier and servant unto his life's end.

This was Ashley's *credo*, the faith by which he lived, not merely the standards he set for a school for his first-born. Anthony went to Rugby, but Francis, the second son, so dearly loved, so joyous and delightful, was sent to Harrow, his father's school, where Ashley had first determined his life's purpose and had vowed to repay by years of service the debt owed by a cruel world to one unknown, suffering man.

VII

The Ten-Hour Day at Last

ROBERT PEEL was a Lancashireman. That meant he was hard-headed and looked facts in the face. He knew that the Corn Laws must go. It remained to educate his party. Graham was with him; Herbert was a sound young man; Gladstone had a genius for finance and would have been a help, but he had just resigned from office through a scruple of conscience over an Irish question. The main difficulty was Stanley. However, there was time. Everything could be done in time.

But the potatoes altered that. In August 1845 all was calm, unusually calm. Then an uneasy rumour got abroad. The potato crop in Kent was suffering from blight; if it spread to Ireland, it would mean famine for that wretched people and little better than famine for the English poor. Unless there was a good harvest. But it rained all September. That settled it. Only one thing could prevent tragic and unparalleled hardships: a prompt and complete repeal of the Corn Laws. Russell asserted it, Peel admitted it, even Ashley, touring Lancashire and Yorkshire and planning a new campaign for the ten-hour day, wrote to his constituents in Dorset advocating gradual abolition. He brought down upon himself a torrent of abuse: from the Anti-Corn-Law League for not going all out for immediate repeal; from his distressed constituents for his apostasy in approving of repeal at all.

At the end of October Peel sounded his Cabinet. Stanley remained firmly against repeal, and early in December Peel resigned. The Queen sent for Russell, but he failed to form a government, ostensibly because Lord Grey would not work with Palmerston. In fact, Russell was not sorry to " hand back the poisoned chalice " to Sir Robert Peel; for the landowning interest was so firmly entrenched at Westminster that whoever took the drastic step of complete and immediate repeal might be committing political suicide. But people were starving and Peel was no coward. He returned to office and Gladstone rejoined him in Stanley's place. Ashley was in a dilemma. His constituents' angry response to his letter showed them to be entirely unaffected by the arguments which had caused Peel and Ashley himself to change their opinions. How then could he still represent their interests? He could not vote against his conscience and oppose repeal; nor could he vote for repeal against the direct wishes of the men who had elected him. Obviously he must resign. Parliament reassembled early in the New Year, and on January 27th Peel made a statement pronouncing himself a convinced Free Trader and saying that the Corn Laws would be duly repealed. Ashley gave himself time to do one more job at Westminster and then he resigned. That job was the introduction of another Ten-Hour Bill.

He spent the spring after his resignation trying to explain the situation to the north-country workmen. It was hard work, physically and mentally. "Monday from London to Manchester, and meeting in the evening. Tuesday to Preston and meeting; Wednesday to dine with Thomas Fielden and meeting at Ashton; Thursday to inspect large madhouse and meeting at Bolton; Friday, Oldham; Saturday to Bradford and dinner with Walker. God grant that Sunday may be quiet. Monday meeting at Bradford; Tuesday, Halifax; Wednesday, Huddersfield; Thursday, Leeds; Friday homeward, God be praised. This is the pertinacious, unwearied revolution of a steam engine."

There was no exultation of spirit to spur on the wearied body; there was only an awkward scruple of conscience to explain to men who were unlikely to share it or to admit that there could be two views about the Corn Laws. No wonder he was tired though "passably successful".

Meanwhile in the Commons his work was carried on by John Fielden, the member for Oldham. He was a rich mill-owner, whose own fortune would be the first to vanish if his

opponents' gloomy prognostications were true and the restriction of hours really meant the collapse of the cotton
trade. But he was ready to stake his profits on the righteousness of his cause, and he pushed forward with the Bill in
his usual energetic way. Like Ashley before him, he found
himself up against Graham, who seemed to think the whole
future of England depended on the girls and boys working
those two extra hours a day.

The second reading was moved on April 29th, 1846, but
after much discussion the debate was adjourned for three
weeks. Ashley haunted the lobbies, and when at length the
vote was taken and the Bill was lost by ten votes he could
be forgiven for feeling that if only he had been in his usual
seat the issue might have been different. The defeat was a
bitter disappointment, but now at long last circumstances
were playing into the hands of the reformers. In June
Peel's Government fell, overturned by the continued hostility
of Stanley and the Tory rebels led in the Commons by Disraeli. Russell took office, and in January 1847 Fielden introduced the Ten-Hour Bill again, this time with the goodwill
of the Government. A general election was imminent and
he generously offered to wait till Ashley had re-entered
Parliament, but the latter would not run the risk such
a delay might entail. So Fielden was left to steer the
Bill through the Commons, not without anxiety when
the compromise of an eleven-hour day was proposed and
the Government hinted its approval. But the amendment
was defeated and on May 3rd the Bill passed its third
reading by one hundred and fifty-one votes to eighty-eight.
After years of struggle the ten-hour day was legally established, and despite the Jonahs, the cotton industry still
survived.

Ashley shared with Fielden a triumphant tour in the
north after Parliament was dissolved, and in the ensuing
election was returned M.P. for Bath. Fielden lost his seat;
with his usual impulsiveness he had declared that young
Cobbett must be his colleague, and Oldham men won't stand
"must" even from a local hero. Two years later he died,

and Ashley was left alone to face new complications and difficulties which arose all too soon to mar the joy of 1847. It became clear that there were ways and means of evading the ten-hour day. By using the relay system, the machines were kept going from five-thirty in the morning to eight-thirty at night and the whole spirit of the Act was jeopardized. The young people were kept hanging about for the whole time and, in the words of Karl Marx, " the hours of rest were turned into hours of enforced idleness, which drove the youths to the pot-houses and the girls to the brothel ". Trade was beginning to revive for a variety of reasons, and prosperous days were succeeding the " hungry forties ". This made it next to impossible to prevent evasions of the Act, especially as test cases had made it clear that the letter of the law was not being broken. But the men who had fought the battle of the factory children were not the sort to let themselves be robbed of the fruits of victory. The Short Time Committees were re-formed, agitations were set on foot, and once more the fight was on.

Ashley was sick at heart. " The work to be done all over again, and I seventeen years older than when I began. But as I did not commence, so neither shall I renew it in my own strength. My sufficiency, if there be any, is of God." But he was not the same man that he had been in 1833 nor in 1843. In the last few years in various ways there had been a change of direction in his life and his interests. Less than ever was he likely to please the stalwarts of Lancashire and Yorkshire.

To begin with he had been eighteen months out of Parliament. During that time he had not been idle. Often during his labour in the House of Commons there had been at the back of his mind the memory of the starving people he passed in the crowded streets. It was, he said, like a bad taste in his mouth. " It cannot be inevitable to have so many poor." He was impelled to find out the facts. And so he took advantage of the freedom from parliamentary duties to explore the slums of London. He was amazed and intensely distressed at what he saw. Man was an immortal spirit and yet he was housed, too often, amid indescribable filth in surroundings that must inevitably deaden every gleam of the divine. What was the good of talking about education and leisure when men and women were living in such conditions? Give them first air, cleanliness, food—then it would be time enough to talk about education. When he was asked to become Chairman of the newly created Central Board of Health he had to agree, though he guessed that the new job would involve "trouble, anxiety, reproach, abuse, unpopularity", and, he should have added, an overwhelming amount of hard day-to-day work. But he did not consider that such duties absolved him from further responsibilities towards the poor. He must get to know them personally, overcome his antipathy to dirty bodies and fetid homes, go and meet them and hold out to them that hand of fellowship which might be the means of lifting them out of the filth and darkness of their existence. All this was borne in upon him as he went down back streets with city missioners and threw himself each year with growing zeal into the work of the ragged schools. When the evasions of the Ten-Hour Act threatened to draw him back into the maelstrom of politics, he felt himself unable to face the tactical battles, the intrigues, the wearisome delays of parliamentary procedure. It was his job to go out and help people; if he never stopped, day and night, for the rest of his life, he would barely do enough to justify himself before God, to excuse himself for living with enough to eat and drink and books to read and comforts to enjoy, while so many other of God's children existed—or died—in the slums.

In the spring of 1849 that happened which robbed him still further of resilience and buoyancy. One evening in May he received a letter from Harrow to say that Francis was seriously ill. He and his wife hurried to the school, where they found the boy fighting a severe attack of pneumonia. Ten days of agony followed. It was a losing battle, but hope dies hard and Ashley rejoiced as he sat

with his son on the evening of June 1st that there were
definite signs of returning strength. Half an hour later he
was recalled to the room; there had been a sudden collapse
and he arrived only in time to see him die. They were
heart-broken. Francis had been everybody's favourite.
During these last ten days he had been so patient, anxious
only about the amount of money his illness was costing his
parents, pleased that so many called to enquire, but that,
he said, was because he was his father's son. They need
not fear for him. " Whatever is God's will is enough for
me," he had said; but for themselves it was as if a light
had been put out. " Every day and every hour bring his
memory to our thoughts, the books, the chair, the things
we so often talked about." Francis was buried in the
churchyard at Harrow, and at the end of the ornate
memorial the parents' grief and faith are enshrined in the
simple words, " Is it well with the child? It is well."
Ashley went on with his work. Every day brought its fill
of business, and there was comfort in the momentary dull-
ing of the pain that came with immersion in practical
affairs. But the man who had to deal with the ten-hour
problem in the next twelve months walked in a darkened
world.

A few weeks after Francis's death two mill-owners called
on Ashley and were received with the courtesy and attention he was ready to give to all men. They discussed a
compromise preferable to the eleven-hour day exclusive
of meals which the Government proposed. The new sug-
gestion was the establishment for protected persons of a
ten-and-a-half-hour day within the limits of 6 a.m. and
6 p.m. (one and a half hours being allowed for meals), and
the cessation of work at 2 p.m. on Saturdays. This scheme
would add two hours to the total in a week, but for this
sacrifice the workers obtained the two great advantages of
a Saturday half-holiday, and the limitation of working
hours to twelve in place of the present range from 5.30 to
8 p.m. Ashley agreed that there was much to be said for
the compromise.

Unfortunately the report of this meeting published in *The Manchester Guardian* gave the impression that he had spoken favourably of the eleven-hour compromise. Nor did his north-country friends like the idea of his colloguing with mill-owners. Oastler, with his vituperative tongue, young Cobbett, who was another extremist, and Fielden's pugnacious relatives all regarded Ashley as suspect, and they were on the spot to influence the operatives. So during the winter and early spring there were many signs of friction. A decision in the Exchequer Court in February 1850, which definitely stated that the use of the relay system was legal under the existing laws, made action imperative. An amending Bill must be introduced in the new session, and the question was who should take charge of it. Ashley wrote to the Short Time Committees offering his services. But the Left Wing had their eye on another champion, Lord John Manners, the Earl of Rutland's son, who had the advantage of being a northerner. There were some distressing meetings and counter-meetings in which the adherents of the two parties suggested respectively that the Bill should be entrusted to Manners, Ashley, and a certain Mr. Bankes, or to Ashley alone with the others' support. It was clear that the latter's hold upon his former colleagues was dwindling. But though he was unutterably tired he went steadily ahead. On March 14th he asked leave in the House to introduce a Bill amending the Act of 1843, upon which the Exchequer judgement had been based. But the amending clause was not satisfactory, and the lawyers who attempted to reframe it declared that no single clause would put the matter right without various new regulations as to meal-times. Nevertheless, he gave notice on April 30th of his intention to move the revised clause. Three days later the Home Secretary, Sir George Grey, announced that the Government intended to introduce a new Bill, based on the ten-and-a-half-hour compromise, the twelve-hour limit to the range of work and the Saturday half-day.

There can be no real doubt that this was the best solution

E

at the moment. Ashley, with his belief in the Puritan Sunday and the stress he laid in consequence on the need for time off on Saturday, saw all the advantages of the Government proposal. The essential thing was the provision of conditions in which young people could live healthy, reasonable lives, and the limitation of the range of working hours was thus extremely valuable.[1] But he made a tactical error in announcing his approval. Instead of consulting the Short Time Committees first, he wrote a letter on May 8th and sent it to *The Times*, announcing his intention of supporting the Government Bill. The publication of the letter on May 9th precluded any further argument and evoked cries of " Traitor " from the bewildered workers. He no doubt meant to prevent discussion, for he feared that delay in accepting the terms would result in the substitution of the eleven-hour compromise, and he expected to be misunderstood, but he was unprepared for the violence and passion of the outcry, the abusive letters in the north-country papers; bitter words from opponents in the House. " I did consider myself their friend," he said, " and I declare before God that I have done that which appeared to me to be the best for their interests. . . . I have sacrificed to them almost everything that a public man holds dear to him, and now I have concluded by giving them that which I prize most of all—I have even sacrificed for them my reputation."

The Bill passed on its gloomy way and became law at the end of the session. Manners did his best for the extremists. He proposed, without any chance of success, that work should stop at 5.30 p.m. instead of 6, and Disraeli made a brilliant speech in his support. Ashley was sadly disillusioned when the Government threw out his amendment including the word " children " in the protective clauses, which as originally framed only referred to young people (the thirteen to eighteen years old). Without the inclusion of the " nine to thirteens " the latter could

[1] See Hutchins and Harrison: *A History of Factory Legislation*, p. 108.

still be used to feed the machines in shifts over the longer range of hours, and the hope of limiting the hours of adult labour was thus destroyed. He proposed his amendment a second time on June 14th and was again beaten, by one vote only. This specific hardship was put right by Palmerston in 1853, and after that date the benefits of the new Act soon became apparent. But it was reserved for Disraeli's Government in 1874, a quarter of a century after it had first been granted them, to give the young workers the ten-hour day by adding an extra half-hour for meals; it seems incredible that so simple a solution was quite unacceptable in 1850 when the bogey of reduction of output still haunted the manufacturers' sleep. In actual fact experience soon showed that fitter workers produced more goods in the shorter hours, a fact to be recalled to-day when the danger of over-long hours has again become a very real menace to society.

Ashley shared with many other pioneers—the elder Peel, Hobhouse, Fielden, Oastler, Wood—the credit of achieving not merely a reduction in hours of labour but indirectly a fresh orientation in legislative activity, a reluctant admission by Westminster and Whitehall that they were concerned with every aspect of life, the well-being and education no less than the safety of the people. Ashley's particular contribution lay in his recognition of the largeness and complexity of the problem. His colleagues' prime concern might be the shortening of the working day, a restriction of motive-power, or the establishment of better working conditions; his object was the production of better people. Women ought to be " protected persons " so that their children should be born healthy and they themselves have time to learn to sew and bake and be good mothers. Children should work less hours so that they could be instructed not only how to read and write but, above all, how to be Christians. His approach to all questions was pragmatic; his immediate concern with whatever was next to be done; but in all his work for factory reform he never lost sight of the goal—which was the same goal towards which he struggled in his work at the Board of Health, in the Ragged Schools, and in every one of his many activities—the gradual emergence of a people, healthy in body, mind and spirit, fit and eager to fulfil the chief end of man, " to glorify God and enjoy Him for ever."

VIII

"*You Are Your Brother's Keeper*"

ARCHBISHOP TEMPLE, writing in 1941, and laying down the prerequisites of a just peace and a new social order, put first the demand that " every citizen should be housed in decency and dignity ". Life is sacramental: it is through the material things of life, our bodies, our homes, our towns, that we express ourselves and establish our relations with our fellows. And since God is the Lord of all life, these material things are of value; our bodies are the temples in which our spirits are housed and our homes the visible signs of the spiritual grace of family affection. As in 1940, so in 1840, the men and women who set out to improve the material conditions of their fellows were, in the main, those who realized the truth of Ashley's dictum that "good drainage, good ventilation, good and healthy houses and an ample supply of cold water" were part and parcel of the job of spreading God's Kingdom, essentials without which education was a farce and moral homilies little better than blasphemy. "The horrible state of our towns and the conditions of the dwellings of many of our people lie at the root of two-thirds of the disorders that afflict our land."[1]

In 1841 Ashley was invited by Dr. Southwood Smith to visit the slums of East London. Southwood Smith, most lovable and upright of men, was physician at the London Fever Hospital. His conviction that epidemics might be prevented by purer air and better sanitation made him a pioneer in the realm of public health. His sweet temper and the spirit in which he worked, that of a man who had been intended for the pulpit and regarded his doctoring with the self-dedication of the priest, made him not only a colleague whom Ashley trusted but a dear and valued

[1] Shaftesbury: *Speeches*. Introduction, p. xi. See also J. Wesley Bready: *Lord Shaftesbury and Social-Industrial Progress* (1926) for the wider aspects of Shaftesbury's work.

friend. He was known in every street and by-way in East
London, sometimes going on foot, often in the cleaner parts
with his little grandchild, Gertrude, in the carriage beside
him. Gertrude's sister, Octavia Hill, owed to her grand-
father her first lessons in the art and science of social welfare. Gertrude, who lived with him as a child, tells in her
memoir of his habit of carrying her downstairs in the small
hours to sleep on the study couch while he worked at one of
his innumerable reports.

It was one of his reports presented to the Poor Law Commissioners in 1840 that brought out exceptionally clearly the
lengths to which overcrowding had gone in London. The
then Secretary of State, the Marquis of Normanby, decided
to investigate himself. Southwood Smith took him to visit
some of the black spots and in February 1841 repeated the
experiment with Ashley. The first introduction to Bethnal
Green and Whitechapel affected Ashley in much the same
way as the pauper's funeral he had witnessed as a boy.
"One whiff of Cowyard, Blue Anchor or Baker's Court out-
weighs ten pages of letter press," he declared. Something
must be done immediately to abolish the back-to-back
houses and to cleanse the stagnant sewers whose vapours
made their insidious way through the crowded rooms in
every narrow street. Two Bills were introduced by Lord
Normanby for this purpose, but they perished in the fall of
Melbourne's Government, and Peel forestalled further action
by appointing a Commission to consider the whole question
of the health of towns.

Two reports of the Commission were published in 1842
and 1844. They recommended that local authorities should
be empowered and encouraged to take measures to improve
the state of their towns, while essential services such as that
of drainage and water-supply were centralized under the
control of a Board of Health. Owing in the main to the
exigencies of the Corn Law crisis, it was four years before
this Board was created. In 1848 it was set up with Lord
Morpeth, a government official, as its Chairman and three
other members, Ashley, Southwood Smith and Chadwick,

the man mainly responsible for the reports and the live wire of sanitary reform. In the realm of public health, Ashley had two associates as enthusiastic and pertinacious as himself. If Southwood Smith shared his Christian faith and vision, Edwin Chadwick equalled him in making a nuisance of himself for the good of others.

Chadwick's name keeps cropping up in the story of nine-teenth-century reform, generally fighting vigorously against ignorance, prejudice or vested interest, and just miss-ing greatness because of a lack of that imagination and sympathy without which no man can be great. He suffered from a civil service type of mind, combined with a double-dose of north-country obstinacy. Yet despite his devotion to bureaucracy on one subject he was by no means cold-blooded. He remarked once to Napoleon III, "Sir, it was said of Augustus that he found Rome brick and left it marble. May it be said of you that you found Paris stink-ing and left it sweet." His secret dream was to do the same for London. He worshipped cleanliness. When he was at the Board of Health, according to *The Times*, "It was a perpetual Saturday night and Master John Bull was scrubbed and rubbed and small tooth-combed till the tears ran into his eyes and his teeth chattered and his fists clenched them-selves with worry and pain." Master John Bull did not like it. He had not been brought up to it, like Chadwick, who had been washed all over every day in the Lancashire farmhouse where his mother defied the encroaching dirt of the coal-mines. In G. M. Young's words " the mainspring of Chadwick's career seems to have been a desire to wash the people of England all over by administrative order ".

"Administrative order" was a new phenomenon in Vic-torian England. The Benthamite theory of government, of which Chadwick was an irreproachably orthodox adherent, stressed the need for experts, who investigated, reported and in due course advised administrative action on all the prob-lems which beset man in his ordinary life, but which had hitherto been regarded as outside the sphere of legislation. The Factory Acts, the first tentative Education Grants, and in 1848 the Board of Health all roused opposition in those who were thereby compelled to alter their ways of living, but they were all facets of " a slow evolution by which, while an aristocratic fabric was quietly permeated with Radical ideas, an individualistic society was unobtrusively schooled in the ways of State control."[1]

The Board of Health only remained in existence for five years, during which time it coped with two outbreaks of cholera and concerned itself with various water, drainage and burial schemes. Shaftesbury (he succeeded his father in 1851) threw himself whole-heartedly into the work, tired himself out in a maze of files and correspondence and made various cross-country walks in the search for suitable reservoirs. The routine character of many of his duties helped him considerably in the months after Francis's death, and the cholera epidemic in the autumn of that same year gave an urgency and poignancy to their labours which enabled him to offer his own sorrow to God as he tried to save others from a like tragedy. The attitude of the public, the apathy and at times the open hostility which greeted their efforts, caused him much grief and perplexity, and when in 1854 Parliament voted that the Board should be discontinued, he felt that after five years of intense and unrewarded labour he had been turned off like a piece of lumber.

Yet something definite had been achieved. A start had been made with the colossal task of giving London and the great industrial towns sanitary arrangements adequate to their needs. Cleanliness had been put upon the map. People might quarrel with the bureaucratic nature of the Board but they could not ignore its existence. In fact its continuance had been rendered unnecessary by the steps local authorities were taking in establishing local boards of health to improve the amenities of their boroughs. Never again would people pretend that open sewers and the absence of lavatories were things that didn't matter!

One of the most valuable contributions Shaftesbury made

[1] G. M. Young: *Victorian England*, p. 47.

to the good causes he supported was his creation of an informed, moderate, yet irresistible, public opinion, which in due course made it not only possible but obligatory for a government to take action. Particularly was this so in regard to housing, the companion subject to sanitation which the Board of Health failed to tackle but upon which Ashley's own energies were concentrated to an increased extent. Obviously the two subjects went together. There could be no health while there was such a complete lack of adequate accommodation for the growing population of London and the industrial towns. In Bradford, for instance, a quarter of the people were said to be housed in impossible conditions. One landlord was fined for letting twenty people sleep in a cellar about four yards square. Children with small-pox lay among the naked men and women. The landlord shrugged his shoulders. "Can I let them lie in the street?" he cried. Even such apparent "improvements" as the building of New Oxford Street had their seamy side. While the well-to-do paraded westward admiring the great new thoroughfare and patronizing the shops, the dispossessed who had lived in the demolished slums were left to fend for themselves in the squalid alleys of Holborn and Bloomsbury. In Church Lane (ironic name!) each small house had a complement of some forty people, living in unimaginable conditions of filth and human degradation. The plague and cholera swept through such quarters like a flame over parched corn, while in model homes near by there were few or no fatalities.

In this matter of housing during the "forties" men were educating opinion through their experiments with model lodging-houses much as their successors to-day experiment in the right use of leisure with clubs and community centres. There was a model lodging-house at George Street, Bloomsbury, another in Streatham Street, one in St. Pancras near to the Fever Hospital established through the efforts of Southwood Smith, who in 1843 helped to found "The Metropolitan Association for Improving the Dwellings of the Industrial Classes". Akin to this was the "Labourer's

Friend Society ", which Ashley had formed in the previous year and which held its first public meeting in '44 under the name of the "Society for Improving the Condition of the Labouring Classes ". All very pompous and Victorian and respectable, and no doubt many of the Labouring Classes had no wish to be improved; yet none the less such movements did represent an honest attempt to make a better world, and it was these voluntary associations which gave drive and vision to the cause they advocated.

In the years between the first visit to Bethnal Green and the creation of the Board of Health, Ashley was working steadily, collecting facts and passing them on to the type of people who joined such societies as these and with whose help alone he could force the hands of the authorities. A wider public was reached through an article in the *Quarterly Review*. Eventually, in 1851, he was able to introduce two Housing Bills into the Commons with a fair chance of success. Both became law in due course and Ashley had the unique experience of sponsoring them in both Houses, for his father died and he entered the House of Lords as the seventh Earl of Shaftesbury during the passage of the Bills. The first empowered local authorities to build and equip lodging-houses for the working classes. It was a permissive Act and remained a dead letter, and Huddersfield alone made use of its enabling powers. Local authorities are not always noticeably enlightened. But the second Bill proved invaluable for it authorized the registration and inspection of lodging-houses already in existence. Dickens declared it to be the best measure ever passed in Parliament, a pardonable exaggeration by one whose whole being burned with indignation at the miseries of the poor, and who had drawn in the pages of *Bleak House* a memorable picture of Tom All Alone's, the home of Jo the crossing-sweeper. Ashley realized how debilitated in every way, in mental and moral stamina as well as in physical energy, the folk became who breathed in the foul gas of the sewers or the stale air of rooms crowded to bursting point. Imagine a room of eighteen feet by ten, occupied by twenty-seven

adults, thirty-one children and their dogs! Those were the
statistics one of his enquiries had elicited! Many a young
man, coming up from the country to work in London, must
have gone to pieces in health and morals simply because
at the start he could find no clean and healthy place in
which to live. Fresh air might well have been included
with water in his mind when Ashley remarked, regarding
the latter, "It is overwhelming, heart-breaking, awful to
reflect how many thousands are deprived in this Christian
city of the prime requisite for health, comfort, decency."

Without decency and dignity, freedom from fear and
want, you could not have good citizens either of London or
of the Kingdom of God. And both as a Christian and as a
statesman, Ashley felt that the creation of good citizens was
an urgent and imperative task. In 1848 all Europe was in
revolution and the Chartist rising agitated England itself.
Ashley did not fear the Chartists so much as the "lazy
ecclesiastics and the prejudiced well-to-do who failed to rise
to their responsibilities". He was convinced that the era of
change initiated by the Reform Bill of 1832 would continue,
and that far-seeing statesmen should concentrate on educating the masses so that they became more fit to exercise the
power that would eventually be theirs. The public bath-
houses, the model dwellings, the working men's institutes
were not "sops" to keep the people quiet but part and
parcel of his wider aim, the building of a true democracy.
Yet neither health, nor housing, nor education were sufficient in themselves. There was yet another element in the
building of a great and united people. There must be personal contact between the haves and the have-nots. You
cannot scrub people clean by administrative order; only
when your heart aches for them will you know how to help
them. He might urge the necessity of legislative action
over an increasingly wide sphere of activity, but he knew
that the gracious flower of community would only flourish
in a state in which, in addition to social justice, there existed between the citizens mutual respect and a personal
sense of responsibility for each other's welfare. And so,

though his activity at Westminster never flagged, he grew steadily more conscious of the need for something else, a chance to express in personal service his consciousness of the debt he owed the poor.

In February 1843 he had seen an advertisement in *The Times* headed "Field Lane Sabbath School". It asked for help in money or service to make permanent an experiment begun two years earlier "for instructing (free of expense) those who, from their poverty or ragged condition, are prevented attending any other place of religious instruction". (Go into any elementary school to-day; rejoice in the sight of bright-eyed boys and girls, neatly dressed, happy and disciplined, with their daily milk and their school dinners, and be ready with your answer next time you meet the man who says there is no progress!) Field Lane was in a district near Holborn Hill, known as Jack Ketch's Warren. It was no unusual sight to see fifty constables with cutlasses marching that way to quell disturbances, but the prime movers thereof usually escaped by means of trap-doors or other secret contrivances giving on to the Fleet Ditch. Ashley wasted no time in visiting the district and making himself known, and before long a Union was formed of the Ragged Schools in London with Ashley as President. They were a mixed crowd, the people who tackled this job. A city missionary and three others, a solicitor's clerk, a woollen draper, and a dealer in second-hand tools; these were the four who first met together and amid the press and bustle of their ordinary lives caught the vision of a great design. Those who helped in the early days, visiting, teaching, finding money, scholars or premises, included Lord Mayors, tinkers, peers and shopkeepers. They were all brothers in Christ; it was a veritable democracy of service. On one occasion Ashley found a barn which he thought would serve as a school. But no one had the money to repair it. So he went to Westminster and stood in Palace Yard, accosting his friends as they passed in and out of the House of Lords. When he had collected twenty-odd pounds he returned triumphant and the work was put in hand.

There were in London a number of children running wild, whose parents were dead or missing and who knew no law nor settled home. They slept under the arches or anywhere else they could find; one discovered that the roller in Regent's Park made an excellent bed. When one's longing for a "comfortable snooze and scrub" became unbearable there was only one thing to do, to be less cute than usual in one's thieving and go for a while to gaol. They earned their living (theoretically) by selling matches, oranges or ballads and by sweeping the crossings. There were, how-ever, ways of augmenting one's income. The teachers at one school noticed that the best scholars slipped away at a fixed hour on Sunday evening. One of them was caught by the master, who said he must wait till the lessons ended. "We must go to business," said the boy; and when asked to explain he cried, "Why, don't you see it's eight o'clock. We must catch them as they come out of the chapels." It was no good pointing out to such boys that theft was sinful and pickpockets might go to Hell. "That may be so," one answered, "but I don't think it can be any worse than this world has been to me."

Four thousand children were attending Ragged Schools in 1848. Their teachers set out to make whole men of these wretched waifs and strays. Teaching them to read and write was the simplest part of the business, teaching them to distinguish between right and wrong was more involved. There could be no doctrinal teaching, for the men of good-will who were working the scheme held many different shades of opinion. But there must be a basis of definite Christian instruction. Otherwise how find an answer to the question, "Why must I do what is right when I want to do what is wrong?" "The Bible should be used in all its integrity." The organizers were content to leave it at that, and many of these sharp-witted children, coming fresh to that grandest of all text-books, as respectable folk so seldom do, found in it the power and beauty to bring their spirits to life. Mean-while they sat half-naked in their rags. That too must be remedied. One teacher divided his class into "tailors" and "shoemakers", and while half made shoes for themselves and their companions, the others—how painfully at first and with what laborious care!—produced clothes for the community.

Such activities necessitated discipline, and that was not easily come by. The first fortnight in a new school was usually pandemonium. When one was opened in Ireland, twenty-four boys, all smoking the largest pipes they could find, took possession of the room and refused to leave it day or night. With equal resolution they refused to learn. Fortunately the teachers kept calm, remembering that nothing is so fatal to a practical joke as lack of response on the part of the victim. The boys grew tired in time and went away and the school went on. Sometimes an individual boy did his best to make a master's life unbearable; one master unwisely lost his temper, seized the offender and shook him. A few moments later the master was prone on the ground, the lad having crawled between his legs and thrown him. The master decided to take no notice, he got to his feet and continued the lesson. The boy's honour was satisfied and there was no more trouble. But such incidents made Ashley and his friends feel anxious when the Government suggested a regular inspection by state officials. They insisted politely but firmly that no inspector could possibly understand their own special difficulties and their way of tackling them. Ragged School teachers were born, not made.

It was not easy to find a niche for these young folk in London, even when they became passably respectable. Ashley's wish was to send many of them to Australia, to man its farms and ranches, and to send out young women to undertake domestic work and become in due time wives and mothers in the new land. Here they could truly begin again with a status and reputation as good as any other. But it needed money. It was hard enough to get sufficient money to run the schools. Most of their financial support came from small shopkeepers. The well-to-do were chary of hobnobbing with dissenters, and they responded without enthusiasm to Ashley's appeals. The Bishop of Norwich, Edward Stanley, was one glorious exception, for he turned up on every occasion to support any cause with which he saw Lord Shaftesbury's name connected.

In 1848 Ashley made an appeal for help to Parliament. He received a grant of fifteen hundred pounds which enabled a start to be made with emigration. It was not easy for the young people who took the plunge. One of the girls wrote to her teacher, " All I wish is that my sister, Susan, had come out with me." And home-sick, she declared, " Though I am thousands of miles from you and all my friends, yet you are always in my mind, and the old wall of the poor-school." But she was one of the lucky ones. She had a good place and a mistress who was " more like a mother to her ". Perhaps later they managed to send Susan out to join her. The boys were tougher; one of them, writing on arrival to his mother, gave her a brief account of Australia: " The blacks are not very wild in the towns but they are out in the Bush where they are wild; they catch kangaroos and eat them. Parrots and cockatoos are very numerous here; the natives will catch them for you and give them to you if you give them a piece of bread or tobacco. I forgot to tell you how much wages I am to receive; it is 12L per year and my rations and washing." How anxiously Shaftesbury must have prayed that, thrown out into the world away from the good influences of the school as well as the bad influences of the streets, his young people might win through to a happy and law-abiding existence. He must have wondered often how it fared with three lads who wrote to him as Chairman of the Union when they were on the point of departure from Gravesend. One of the boys, aged sixteen, lived in a pigsty and had been seven times in prison when he first went to a Ragged School. His ambition in life was to get abroad, and his only chance of fulfilling this ambition to stage a big enough robbery to get himself transported. Both the other boys lived by stealing and begging; one of them kept himself alive by eating rotten apples in the Borough Market. Now with life miraculously changed they wrote to Ashley, "May God bless your Lordship, may God bless Mr. Nash and every Ragged School teacher, and we beg one favour of you, that you will open more schools, such as Mr. Nash's dormitory at Westminster, for there are many poor boys that would be very glad to get in them, and we do promise, through God's grace, to conduct ourselves with the strictest propriety, and open a Sunday school in Australia. You said you would pray for us, so we will for you, every day of our lives, and tell the people in Australia what kind friends you are to poor boys." Perhaps Ashley was able to do so much more than ordinary men, because he was sustained by the prayers of hundreds of humble people whom he had helped in every part of the world.

Every year that passed with its frustrations and its toil made him more conscious of the peace and joy he drew from the Ragged School work. Here he was at his best, free from repressions, shyness or arrogance. He loved the folk he helped, and the men and women who helped him to help. There was John MacGregor (Rob Roy they called him) who enlisted a Shoe Black Brigade of Ragged School urchins to shine the shoes of the foreigners who came over to the Great Exhibition. There was Quintin Hogg who started the Polytechnic after learning the art of training young hooligans under the ægis of the Ragged Schools. There were moments of triumph, such as that of 1854, when Pam, always a ready convert to the progressive schemes he was too busy to think out for himself, passed the Youthful Offenders Act, which extended the work of the Reformatory Schools. Or again, twelve years later, when the Government gave Shaftesbury the use of H.M.S. *Arethusa* and he had the joy of seeing his boys grow into useful citizens nearer at hand than in the antipodes. And as his love for the under-dog grew with the years, there were the costermongers, the parents of so many of his scholars, whose vagrant hearts he won and to whom he turned for the comfort that simple folk alone can give in his hour of greatest sorrow. Many happy evenings were spent at Golden Lane, where a Post Office clerk had devoted his spare time to establishing a mission for the costers. Shaftesbury became its President, joined the Barrow and Donkey Club, and lent his own barrow with the Shaftesbury arms engraved upon it to any costermonger who had not yet saved enough to buy one for himself. In return they gave him a donkey which he christened Coster and took to St. Giles for the grandchildren to play with.

That was one side of the picture. The other was the letters, interviews, chairs, boards, speeches that evoked from him the cry, "I am worn, worn, worn by them all." Sheer hard work, unceasing prayer, hours of nervous conflict when he did not see his way clearly, the willing sacrifice of place and fortune: these were the gifts he could bring to the service of the people and win in return a deepening peace of mind and, as he looked back over fifty years, the proud cry, "*Sursum corda.*"

F

IX

The Golden Fifties

THE sixth Earl of Shaftesbury died in June 1851, and on the twenty-third of that month, the seventh Earl, leaving behind that name which he had borne with honour during twenty-five years of public life, took his seat in the House of Lords. He did not react kindly to the new surroundings for despite his lack of close party connections he was a House of Commons man. He knew its rules, its traditions, the fascination of bending it to one's will, one's impotence when a thinning House and the ticking of the clock made a mockery of one's hopes. He knew everybody: Johnny Russell, the thin-lipped Graham, the Manchester veterans and the younger men, Dizzy whom he distrusted but who at least had written *Sybil,* and young Gladstone, who held the pernicious doctrines of the Tractarians but had a conscience and a nose for facts as keen as his own. " Everything of importance revolves round the centre of the Commons' House; unless you be there to see it, hear it, feel it you get it at second hand, and then only half." And now he found himself among the Peers. " It seems no place for me; a Statue Gallery, some say a Dormitory. . . . Shall I ever be able to do anything? " But he had to make the attempt. His first task was to sponsor one of his own Housing Bills. As on the first occasion when he had spoken in the Lower House, his voice was low and his manner unprepossessing, but his hearers thought none the worse of him for these signs of nervousness and, pleased to pay a compliment to a new colleague whose reputation was well-established among them, the Lords passed the measure after a brief debate. Shaftesbury missed the savour of his successes in the Commons, but on June 30th, just a week after his first appearance, he " broke cover in a bit of humanity-mongering about Chimney Sweeps ". " Found my voice . . ." he notes in his Diary, "was well received; thanked God and took courage." When his second Housing Bill was welcomed with cheers he was delighted. He was going to be a success. His diffidence, which was partly pride, gave place to a rare good humour. There could not fail to be a certain attraction in the pomp and circumstance of the Upper House, not least to one like himself so conscious of the functions of a true aristocracy. On August 8th he wrote, "Day fine; everything gay and good-humoured. Attended (the prorogation) as a peer and enraptured the Chancellor and Law Lords by wearing the robes of the first Lord Shaftesbury."

One reason in particular he had for satisfaction. Now at last he was master at Wimborne St. Giles. He spent the summer in typical fashion, learning the facts about the people whose well-being was now directly his care. He spent the autumn going through his father's papers, taking stock of his financial position and deciding that he could never afford with his large family and many commitments to live in the ancestral home he loved so dearly. "There are things here to make one's flesh creep, and I have not a farthing to set them right," he cried in anguish. He tried to do something immediately with borrowed money, and a year or so later obtained funds by selling some of the family pictures. The repair of the parish church and the provision of schools in the hitherto unlettered villages was an expensive but comparatively simple job; it was less easy to cope with the overcrowding. On September 6th the Diary reads, "Shocking state of cottages; stuffed like figs in a drum. Were not the people as cleanly as they can be we should have an epidemic. Must build others, cost what it may." One thing he could do at once to ease the labourers' lot, and that was to forbid the practice of payment in kind in which the farmers had been indulging as unscrupulously as did the coal-owners up north. The "truck system" was stamped out once for all at St. Giles, though some of Shaftesbury's tenants threw up their farms rather than obey his orders. Finally, he put in hand certain drainage schemes, and then returned to London, leaving his agent Waters in charge and conscious that he had done no more than attack the fringe of the problem. Next spring he moved from Brook Street to the family house in Grosvenor Square, where the rest of his life was spent in between visits to the Continent, happy holidays at Broadlands, and the few precious weeks every year at St. Giles.

His family was growing up. Anthony had joined the Navy in 1849, shortly before Francis's death. A few years after his father became a Peer he entered the House of Commons as M.P. for Hull. Maurice, the next boy, was an invalid, but Evelyn was doing well. He left Harrow in 1855 and went to study at Geneva. Lionel was still at school, and Cecil, the youngest boy, was a baby. In between were the four girls, Victoria, whom they called Vea, Mary, a sweet but delicate girl who was happiest when she was teaching in the infant school at St. Giles, Constance and Edith (little " Hilda ") who was still in the nursery with Cecil. Lady Shaftesbury remained the same whatever her rank, tired now in body but not in spirit, wearing herself out in smoothing the tangles of her husband's crowded days, doing all she could to ease the suffering of the feeble Maurice, watching Mary and Constance anxiously, looking after the children, rejoicing in her sons' grown-up achievements, never complaining of being short of money and somehow managing to be happy all the time.

When Evelyn returned from Geneva he became secretary to Lord Palmerston. The connection between the two families was drawn yet closer, and their friendship deepened as the young man shared increasingly the interests and affections alike of his father and of his employer. These were the years of Palmerston's apotheosis. He had been in uneasy occupation of the Foreign Office in the Whig Government which succeeded that of Peel. But the Queen disliked him and he disliked the French and there was constant friction, in marked contrast to his masterly handling of the Belgian situation ten years earlier. An observer might well have thought that Pam was past his prime. At length, in December 1851, he overstepped the mark by a personal expression of approbation for Louis Napoleon's *coup d'état*. This gave Russell the chance to get rid of his difficult colleague. Pam went out of office much chagrined. But within a month or two he had given Russell the " tit for tat ", and engineered his defeat on an unimportant motion. Stanley (now Lord Derby) succeeded Russell but failed to pass his budget. A coalition of Whigs and Peelites came next with Aberdeen, honest and incompetent, at its head, Russell as leader of the Lower House and Palmerston as Home Secretary. But it only succeeded in blundering into the Crimean War and Russell, who hated the war and whose ambition was to introduce a new measure of reform, was miserable and uncertain. At last he resigned and the Government fell to pieces. The country heard with dismay of the horrors of Sevastopol. Soldiers were dying in their thousands while the so-called leaders of the people were stricken, it seemed, with paralysis. In the dark winter of 1854-5 Palmerston rose to the occasion, became Prime Minister at the age of seventy and won the undying love of the common people by his energy and cheerfulness and his faith in England's future.

Against this political background, the country moved into a new phase of its being. The Crimea proved at its worst a tragic interlude. The mood of 1851 returned, the year of the Great Exhibition when England's stability and economic well-being stood out in marked contrast to the distraught state of Europe. The dominant figure at Windsor was the Prince Consort, under whose severe though loving tutelage Victoria had developed from the self-willed, selfish young Queen into the perfect wife and mother, whose whole kingdom was her family. Albert's desire to do good was manifesting itself in many ways, from attendance at the annual meetings of numerous philanthropic societies to the dream of a great cultural centre in Kensington where the youth of London might pursue truth and beauty while their evangelical brethren were achieving goodness in the slums. Evangelicanism itself was on the wane, though the impulse to fight for social righteousness which it had given to the Church still bore fruit in the lives of countless of the laity. But many of the clergy were attracted by the new intellectual forces of the age to a different approach to religion, either historical and æsthetic or analytic and modernist. They were " high " or " broad " rather than " low ". The doctrine of perfectibility and the idea of progress were abroad in the eighteen fifties, culminating in the writings of Darwin and Mill who viewed the story of mankind as a great advance from the ape to the angel, and placed Utopia not too far round the corner. Faced by the challenge of a new generation, those who believed in revealed religion, if they did not always fit easily into the temper of the times, placed their church in a historical setting, revered her Catholic heritage and so linked up with the sense of continuity and progress. As for the modernists, only one thing was missing from their armoury of moral and spiritual weapons—a sense of sin. Man stood upright, his eyes fixed on the distant horizon, and thanked God for the gift of reason, his clear sight and the strength of his hands. Only a few, like Shaftesbury, were old-fashioned enough to believe that there was one problem the moderns failed to recognize, a problem enshrined in Paul's anguished exclamation, " For the good that I would I do not; but the evil which I would not, that I do."

Somehow things went wrong, and after the Victorian age of achievement, that century of hope, came class warfare, the totalitarian state, the holocausts of 1914 and 1939 and the world's despairing cry: " God be merciful to me a sinner."

But in the early fifties even Shaftesbury could not escape from a sense of the possibilities of life. During these years his interests had widened. He travelled increasingly on the Continent. His wife liked it and it gave him the breathing-space and the time for reading and reflection which he never found at home. He had been on the verge of a breakdown. The frustrations and misunderstandings which had

clouded the end of the Ten-Hour struggle; the tragedy of
Francis's death and the iron control he had placed upon
himself; the strain of his work at the Board of Health and
the contacts with filth and wretchedness which it imposed
upon him; and finally the gigantic tasks of coping with his
new responsibilities at St. Giles combined to reduce him to
a state of nervous and physical exhaustion. In addition
there was his work on the Lunacy Commission, always exacting and frequently distressing, and the Ragged School
duties which meant not only the refreshing hours he spent
among the boys and girls but the organization of meetings
to win financial support and much speech-making, in this
and other good causes, which never came easily to Shaftesbury. No wonder his son Evelyn, whose companionship
steadily became more precious, asked him in one of his
letters how he did it. His father replied, " You ask me how
I get through so much work; why, as I hope that you will
hereafter, by hearty prayer to Almighty God before I begin,
by entering into it with faith and zeal, and by making my
end to be His glory and the good of mankind."

At length Nature called a halt. In June '52 his doctor
ordered him to Ems to drink the waters, and in the ensuing
years he acquired the habit of one or two visits to the Continent each year. Being the sort of person he was, he soon
became interested and agitated about the things he found
there, nosing out injustices like a hound on the scent. When
two shopkeepers in Florence were converted to Protestantism
and in consequence were condemned to the galleys by a
fanatical Grand Duke of Tuscany, outraged opinion in England took it for granted that Shaftesbury was the man to
champion their cause. He had reached the stage of packing
his bag and was on the point of departure to Italy when the
diplomats stepped in and suggested a more cautious
approach. There were obvious dangers in having a Shaftesbury running wild on the Continent; it was as bad as having
his father-in-law at the Foreign Office. The constant stream
of refugees who came to England from a troubled Europe
were always sure of a welcome at the house in Grosvenor

Square. Nor did it stop short at a welcome in words. One
visitor told him of a heart-rending case and Shaftesbury
was distressed beyond measure because he had no money
available for its immediate relief. Suddenly he remembered
something, went from the room and returned in triumph
with five pounds he had hidden in the library for just such
an emergency as this. As time went on and Italy moved into
the forefront of politics, some felt that Palmerston as Prime
Minister was influenced too easily by the information,
usually the sum of many rumours, which came to him via
Shaftesbury's home, " a house of call for refugees ". And
indeed how could Shaftesbury harden a heart that had
never yet been hardened against the silent, hopeless plea
for sympathy and understanding of these people without
roots.

But he never forgot that his first duty was to the children.
In 1853 he introduced a Bill in the Upper House which he
hoped might remedy the evil of youngsters begging in the
streets. It gave magistrates power to commit the children
to the workhouse, and it is not surprising that the Commons
dropped the measure feeling that it would prove too harsh
in operation. Palmerston carried the Youthful Offenders
Act next year which improved matters considerably, but the
vast problem of juvenile delinquency needed originality and
brilliance in attack and fundamental changes in social conditions such as none has yet achieved.

There was still much to be done for the children in industry, in the brickyards and in the gangs of field workers
scattered over the countryside. There were the women too,
seamstresses, dressmakers, flower-sellers in the streets; while
all these were still unprotected by law, Shaftesbury had
vowed that he would not take office. But now that his
friendship with Palmerston brought him in close touch with
party politics again, he could not help brooding upon what
he was giving up. The rich young man of the Gospels surrendered his possessions no more easily than Shaftesbury his
political ambitions. In 1854 a new temptation assailed him
when Aberdeen wrote to him, asking permission to submit

his name to the Queen for the vacant Blue Ribbon of the Order of the Garter. He refused, and this was one of the few occasions on which the devoted Minnie differed from her husband. She knew that the Queen would be offended, but neither the fear of royal displeasure nor his wife's un-expressed disapproval could overcome Shaftesbury's reluc-tance to accept rewards while so many still dwelt in misery. There was also a practical difficulty. Acceptance would entail fees amounting to one thousand pounds which he could not produce without neglecting his duty to his children and St. Giles.

Early in the following year, another such decision was forced upon him. Palmerston, forming his government in '55, a ticklish business of balancing Whigs and Peelites, stopped being judicious for a moment and on an impulse of affection offered Shaftesbury the Duchy of Lancaster and a seat in his Cabinet. But before the day was out he had withdrawn the offer, for he had found it essential to offer the post to a Whig. Shaftesbury had written a long letter of reluctant acceptance, pointing out the matters on which he must preserve independence of judgement, and he sent it to Palmerston with the half-humorous comment, "You may see that probably after all I may not be such a colleague as you wished for, at least not one worth struggling for. . . ." Of course he felt in his heart that Palmerston should have struggled for him. One half of him wanted to be forced to take office, while the other half dreaded it. It was excruci-ating to be continually tempted and then be cheated of the reward. A month later the Duchy of Lancaster was again vacant and a second time it was offered to Shaftesbury. His wife urged him to accept, but despite her pleadings, he de-murred, "I could not satisfy myself that to accept office was a divine call: I was satisfied that God had called me to labour among the poor."

Most certainly he was right. Such speeches as he made on foreign politics in the Lords, his support of Palmerston over the "Arrow" incident a few years later, his opposition to Reform at home, all indicate that as a statesman he would have made at least as many mistakes as his colleagues. But at the moment with his Queen, his wife, his friend all urging acceptance, it seemed impossible to refuse. Palmerston was in a hurry: Shaftesbury was instructed to appear at the Palace if he accepted, " to be sworn in at a quarter to three ". He ordered his carriage and went to his room to dress. Still undecided he knelt down and prayed for counsel, wisdom and understanding. There was a knock at the door. He expected it to be word that the carriage was ready, but instead a servant brought him a pencilled note from Palmerston, " Don't go to the Palace." " That was thirty years ago," Shaftesbury wrote as an old man, " but I dance with joy at the remembrance of that interposition as I did when it happened." By his lightness of heart he knew it was the right decision, and it seemed to him that he had received a divine lead. Palmerston had found a Whig ready to take the vacant place, and knowing how Shaftesbury was suffering, he hastened to remove the pressure he had put upon him. Only once again was Shaftesbury offered government rank, by Lord Derby in 1866. But then there was no longer the pull of personal friendship, and he answered without hesitation that it was impossible to accept while one hundred and forty thousand women and children were still outside the scope of the Factory Acts. It was perhaps a somewhat grandiloquent reply, but the root of the matter was just there, the task God had set him was to work for the underdog, not to plan politics nor administer the State. And certainly Pam and Derby escaped a most uneasy colleague.

While these matters were under debate in 1854 an incident occurred which showed clearly where Shaftesbury's true genius lay. One day, at the Board of Health, a visitor called to see him, a certain doctor who had been engaged on a study of cholera in the West Indies. Their conversation turned upon the terrible state of the soldiers in the Crimea. Shaftesbury got down at once to the crucial point: could anything be done about it? In that conversation he and Dr. Gavin worked out between them a scheme for a Sanitary Commission. With some difficulty, for a philanthropist was

suspect, Shaftesbury obtained an interview with Lord Panmure, the Minister of War, and set about organizing an
expedition to go out at once to the Middle East " to purify
the hospitals, ventilate the ships and exert all that science
can do to save life where thousands are dying, not of their
wounds but of dysentery and diarrhœa, the result of foul
air and preventible mischiefs ". Dr. Gavin, who lost his
life in the Crimea, took with him in the party various inspectors and engineers and medical men drawn from the
staff of the Liverpool Town Council. Shaftesbury worded
the commission (" the diction is such that, in housekeeper's
language, it may be said to have bustled the servants "), and
harried Panmure over details of shipping so successfully
that the expedition was at sea within a few days of the
original conversation. Florence Nightingale, already embarked upon her immortal labours, said later that it saved
the British Army. The whole incident illustrates admirably
Shaftesbury's method of attack. First a sympathetic hear-
ing of the facts; then a discussion as to what it was possible
to do and how it should be done; then an intense concentration upon every detail, using to the full at every stage his
own time and energy and spiritual power.

X

Things of the Spirit

THE Crimean War was ended. After twenty years of strenuous living, England entered thankfully "the deep central calm of the nineteenth century", the prosperous middle years for Shaftesbury as for his country. In September 1855 Maurice, his invalid son, had been released by death from an existence that only his own sweet temper had made bearable. The other sons were doing well, and Anthony had established himself at St. Giles, winning the deepening affection of the tenants and the village folk. Sometimes he appeared beside his father on a public platform, which gave the Earl much joy. The latter was more settled in mind and body than he had been for many years. The final surrender of his political ambitions removed a main cause of that mental restlessness from which he had never been entirely free; the pressure of work which was exhausting him physically had been lessened, much as he regretted it, by the abolition of the Board of Health in 1854, and his life was enriched by the ripening of two deep friendships that put an end effectively to the feeling of loneliness which had often assailed him in youth. The one was with a certain Mr. Haldane, the editor of an Evangelical newspaper, with whom he was in the closest touch until his friend's death shortly before his own. The other was with the Prime Minister, whose stimulating companionship saved the years from the blight of middle-aged complacency.

Shaftesbury, even yet, was not quite sure what to make of Palmerston. He loved him but he found it hard to forgive his variableness. "Hold fast that which is good" was a text dear to Shaftesbury's heart, but his father-in-law held fast to nothing. He was always ready to go full tilt for what seemed to him right at the time, but he was too subtle, he wandered far from the simple policy that Shaftesbury had put into words, " What is morally right can never be politically wrong, and what is morally wrong can never be politically right." Over one matter in particular the Earl was perturbed. He wrote to Evelyn, " I much fear that Palmerston's ecclesiastical appointments will be detestable. He does not know, in theology, Moses from Sydney Smith. The Vicar of Romsey, where he goes to church, is the only clergyman he ever spoke to. . . ." " Why, it was only a short time ago that he heard, for the first time, of the grand heresy of Puseyites and Tractarians." Fortunately, however, Pam had plenty of shrewd wisdom. He did not know much about theology, but he did know a good Christian when he saw him. He entrusted the ecclesiastical appointments almost entirely to Shaftesbury, who during the ensuing years became known as the Bishop-Maker. His appointments in one way were unconventional for he recommended good practical men rather than scholars, distrusting the experience gained " in musty libraries and easy chairs ". The Prime Minister backed him up. When Shaftesbury suggested " a person of no social account ", " What does that signify? Is he the proper man? " was the reply. " Yes, a very proper man." " Then he shall be appointed." This was excellent, so far as it went. But alas! All the Bishop-Maker's " proper men " turned out to be Evangelicals, and when after various ups and downs Palmerston made friends with the Peelites, he found that their leader Gladstone was a staunch Tractarian. The Prime Minister was faced with angry looks from his new colleagues and found that it was due to their dislike of Shaftesbury's bishops. He appealed to him to be cautious : " fit men " of course must be chosen, but when possible not too displeasing to the High Church party. The Earl curbed his enthusiasm, and in the main his nominees justified his choice. They were worthy without being very distinguished, and they were sound in life as well as in doctrine.

Shaftesbury's opinions had mellowed in middle years. To the surprise of his Low Church friends he refused to oppose the endowment of a Chair of Greek at Oxford because a Modernist (Dr. Jowett) was to occupy it. And when Bishop Colenso was deposed from the See of Natal for a critical study of the Book of Deuteronomy, Shaftesbury strongly deprecated the action. But on one point he was adamant. He was Chairman of the Lord's Day Observance Society, and woe betide any who attacked the sanctity of the Puritan Sabbath! In 1849 he succeeded, for a few weeks only, in quashing Sunday posts; later he urged the Sunday closing of Public Houses; in 1856 he was involved in a more serious controversy over the question of bands in the parks. Palmerston had given leave to a Commissioner of Works to introduce the innovation of music in the parks on Sunday, but overpersuaded by Shaftesbury he eventually withdrew the permit. Shaftesbury made no claim to interfere with the individual's liberty of choice; his objection to the bands was based on the fact that their employment was a government act and would therefore give official recognition to the change in practice. Nor did he fail to recognize that all men need fresh air and sport and music, and as patron of the Early Closing Association did much to obtain these benefits for shop assistants and the like. "I believe," he wrote, "there is no other way in which you can improve the observance of the Sabbath so effectually as by giving a half-holiday every Saturday afternoon." By such means only could Sunday be saved from deteriorating into a frantic search for enjoyment rather than a time to pause and recall the eternal things hidden beneath the din and bustle of day-to-day living.

It would be idle to deny, however, that in many ways his Evangelical approach gave Shaftesbury a narrow vision. He was deeply involved in the Ritualist controversy, bringing in an abortive Vestments Bill and spending much time and trouble over an unsatisfactory attempt to reform the ecclesiastical courts. He failed entirely to grasp the wider issues involved in the Oxford Movement whose supporters claimed that it had saved the Church from an individualism that was in danger of becoming too intense. It restored a sense of historical continuity and of beauty and reality to worship without which Anglicanism would have been hard put to it to face the assaults of the new rationalist philosophy. He may have begun to be vaguely conscious of this as the new spirit abroad in the sixties made it clear in what direction the real challenge to orthodoxy lay. Certainly, he drew nearer to his old friend Pusey, and over such matters as the appointment of Bishop Temple in 1869, the two old fighters joined together to oppose the insidious encroachments of the Modernists. On one occasion Shaftesbury went so far as to describe Seeley's *Ecce Homo* as " the most pestilential book ever vomited from the jaws of Hell ". Afterwards he did not remember using the words, but he did not withdraw them. It was at once his strength and weakness that at sixty-odd he could still be moved so deeply, when so many by the balancing of countless phrases have reduced themselves to inanition. But it was not given to him to realize that God's truth may be reached by many different paths, and any approach that seemed to him to impugn the faith of Christ crucified was indeed anathema.

Being what he was, he was bound to have no sympathy with the intellectual subtleties of the Modernists, and little with the æsthetic aspirations of the Tractarians. His true religion is to be found in the words he spoke when he went to Liverpool in 1859 as President of the Social Service Congress. " When people say we should think more of the soul and less of the body, my answer is that the same God who made the soul made the body also. . . . I maintain that God is worshipped, not only by the spiritual, but by the material creation. . . . Our bodies, the temples of the Holy Ghost, ought not to be corrupted by preventible disease, degraded by avoidable filth, and disabled for His service by unnecessary suffering." This was the intensely practical faith in which he lived.

It was the more unfortunate that he failed to achieve fellowship with a group of men who were devoting dedicated lives to the service of their brothers, and whom he

should surely have recognized as his fellow workers with
God.   The greatest tragedy of his life was his failure to
appreciate and co-operate with the Christian Socialists.
Frederick Denison Maurice was not more than a year or
two younger than Shaftesbury; he possessed the same restless exacting conscience, a distrust of his own powers
especially in the sphere of social relationships, unswerving
integrity and a burning love for his fellow men.   Alike in
so many ways and bound by a loyal discipleship to the
same Master, how came it that they could not agree?
Maurice's was the sweeter nature and the finer intellect;
Shaftesbury's melancholy was combined with a certain
harshness and arrogance, inherited traits which Christian
discipline could subdue but not uproot.   Hence came the
difficulty of agreement, intensified by the different environment of their youth.   The Evangelical framework of his
faith saddled Shaftesbury with a creed, less enlightened
than that which his own life proclaimed.   The intense preoccupation of the Calvinists with the soul's salvation (" so
much about us, so little about God," as Maurice put it) had
driven them back upon themselves and lessened, till the
balance was righted, their potency in good works.   But
Maurice had grown up in a gracious and enlightened
Unitarian household.   He himself had embraced the
orthodox faith, feeling that only a full recognition of God's
revelation of Himself in the person of Jesus Christ, made
sense of life or made it possible to uphold, among all the
changes and chances of the world, an unwavering belief in
the absolute love of God.   And this to him was the all-
important fact: that God is love and light and those who
follow Him have life and have it more abundantly.   He
proclaimed the reality of eternal life here and now for
those who live in fellowship with God, though he lost his
professorship at King's College for his unorthodoxy in
doing so!

This Johannine approach to theology was distrusted in
his day, and Maurice was as whole-hearted as Shaftesbury,
sometimes perhaps as cantankerous, in saying precisely

what he believed. "I was sent into the world," he proclaimed, "that I might persuade men to recognize Christ
as the centre of their fellowship with each other," and in
the interest of this fellowship he opposed all controversy
at times so vehemently that he provoked the very thing he
wished to crush. Unfortunately his first contact with
Shaftesbury was on this very point. In 1843 he heard that
the latter was about to organize a petition to the Government urging that action should be taken against the
Tractarians. Maurice at once wrote to Ashley, as he then
was, indicating the right and wrong ways of supporting
Protestantism, sketching the way in which the High
Church party had evolved, deprecating squabbles between
any churchmen in the then state of the country, and
urging Ashley "not to give up to a party what was meant
for mankind, his own noble philanthropic efforts".[1] The
letter had no effect!

The two men never came in closer contact, although
five years later, when the cholera epidemic was turning
Ashley's hair grey at the Board of Health, Maurice and
a group of young friends, who had already adopted the
name of Christian Socialists, were welding themselves into
a closer fellowship in their practical labours in the East
End. The group had come into being through the efforts
of a brilliant young lawyer, J. E. Ludlow, who had experienced the Revolution in Paris in 1848 and dreamed of
transplanting to England some of Louis Blanc's schemes
of co-operative socialism. At his first meeting with
Maurice, it seemed to Ludlow that the gentle clergyman
of Lincoln's Inn lacked drive and dynamic power, but
closer acquaintanceship soon showed him his mistake, and
a deep and lasting friendship sprang up between the two.
They found an ally in Charles Kingsley with his literary
gifts and his robust superabundant genius, and later they
were joined by Tom Hughes, sportsman and gentleman,
author of *Tom Brown's Schooldays*, and the perfect
example of a Christian man of the world. At first the

[1] Maurice: *Life*, I, p. 343.

G

group concerned themselves with propaganda, but from *Politics to the People* they turned to the practical task of caring for the victims of the cholera, and a year or two later they embarked on their great experiment in co-operative associations, in which tailors, cobblers and the like voluntarily banded themselves together to share profits and run their business on a basis of Guild Socialism. They were doomed to failure in part because of the imperfections of their own members, in part because public opinion was not yet ripe for it; but it was an honest attempt to right by Christian methods a problem with which we are still wrestling to-day; how to retain individual enterprise while preventing the exploitation of individual men.

Maurice himself had a dread of committees and organizations and all the paraphernalia of business; perhaps one is not sufficiently grateful for the fact that Shaftesbury could stomach these things and so was able to accomplish so much. Maurice was disheartened by the inability of men to live as brothers, and even as Shaftesbury turned from legislative activity to philanthropy, so Maurice was driven back upon the necessity for individual enlightenment. In 1854 he embarked on the Christian Socialists' most lasting enterprise, the Working Man's College originally opened in Red Lion Square. The house in Red Lion Square had previously been an East End Needlewomen's Workshop. Shaftesbury's interest had been solicited when this latter scheme was set on foot and he was included in the Committee upon which Maurice would not sit because his name and Kingsley's were " likely to disgust Lord Shaftesbury and his friends ". Perhaps because of the rift between the two parties the enterprise was soon abandoned. We must deplore this inability of two great minds who thought alike in so many things (even in their views of democracy!) to recognize their own affinity. Personality, all the tricks and mannerisms with which the body decks itself out, social position, superficial prejudices, all count for so much more in the casual encounters of this world than those fundamental principles and ideals which are our real selves. Pusey and Shaftesbury, parted though they were for years, were kinsmen and knew each other's language and were never so far apart as Maurice and Shaftesbury, two seekers after righteousness, who in their different ways—the one diffusing light, the other power, the one making men think, the other getting things done —revealed perhaps more clearly than any of their contemporaries God's will at work in a sinful world.

Among the most valuable of Shaftesbury's "religious activities" (his "religion" was part and parcel of everything he did) were the Sunday evening services held under his direction, at first at Exeter Hall and later in various London theatres. The Exeter Hall meetings, attended at times by as many as three thousand working or middle-class folk, not habitually church or chapel goers, had been a real force in the country before, in 1857, they were stopped owing to an injunction issued by the local parish priest. A few years later the theatre services began, and Shaftesbury had few happier hours than those he spent at the Victoria Palace reading the Scriptures to a crowded audience, who were a little uncertain about such details as the tunes of the hymns and when one knelt or stood, but who lost themselves at last in the great discovery of the good news of Christ revealed in the lovely words of the English Bible.

During the ten years of Palmerston's premierships, Shaftesbury's Diaries are scanty, as if he were too immersed in the main current of public life to indulge overmuch in self-communings. His work for the children inside Parliament and out continued unabated, while the larger world pressed in upon him, demanding his attention and imposing on him new decisions and emotional experiences. The *Arrow* incident of '57, when the British authorities made use of a doubtful case to press their claims on China, showed him less sure of right and wrong than usual. He distrusted

the motives of those who moved the vote of censure on the
Government, and felt himself bound in loyalty to support
Palmerston. It was the one instance in his career when
he put personal feelings before his principles. Though he
followed up his vote by an inconvenient motion condemn-
ing the opium trade and demanding an enquiry, yet his
support of Palmerston on this occasion, influenced in part
by his belief that it was good for England that Shaftesbury
should continue to appoint England's bishops, shows him
to have been as fallible as the rest of mankind—and perhaps
for that reason is not entirely to be regretted! In his zeal
for the Italian cause and Garibaldi's great crusade, he was
for once on the side of the majority. In America the
struggle to free the slaves roused in Shaftesbury's heart
those warm feelings of indignation against cruelty which he
felt in all cases of oppression near and far. He had read
with deep emotion *Uncle Tom's Cabin*, another of the novels
that worked wonders in the mid-nineteenth century, and he
was soon at his old task of organizing and canalizing the
vague public opinion in this country against slavery; working so zealously that an angry slave-owner in the Southern
States in 1853 asked impatiently who this unknown lordling
might be, "Where was he when Lord Ashley was nobly
fighting for the Factory Bill, and pleading the cause of the
English slave? We never even heard the name of this Lord
Shaftesbury then."

Though no one dominant interest such as the factory
struggle gave unity to Shaftesbury's life at this time, he
worked incessantly and often worked too hard, as is shown
by such entries in the Diary as that of March 28th, 1857:
"Sit down and weep over the sad, wearisome, useless expen-
diture of time and strength on the letters I must write. Have
now at least a hundred letters unanswered. My mind is as
dry as a gravel road, and my nerves are sensitive and harsh
as wires." What he needed of course was a good private
secretary, but he could never afford one. The continual
struggle to make ends meet, his inability to ease his own
path, even to the extent of buying a good book when he saw

one, is a factor that must have contributed much to the
burden he was never quite able to shake from his back. It
was impossible for him to give the necessary attention to his
affairs at St. Giles, where his agent Waters was involved in
an elaborate drainage scheme and was playing fast and loose
with his master's money. The shrewd Palmerston saw what
was happening and tried to warn his son-in-law, but again
the shadow of death was upon Shaftesbury's household, and
it was hard to approach him. Mary, his second daughter,
had for some time been suffering from tuberculosis, and in
1861 she died, after an agonizing year in which her mother
fought fiercely and intensely a losing battle with death.

Soon afterwards Shaftesbury took his wife abroad in the
hope that she might recover some resilience, and Palmerston
set himself to think of some way to give them new hope
and courage on their return. What he did was typical of
the generous, large-hearted man. In December he wrote to
Shaftesbury: "There is one of the vacant Garters which has
not yet been allotted. I very much wish you would take it,
I am sure that its being given you would gratify the whole
country." He hinted that the "fees" difficulty could be
overcome, "an arrangement made with the Treasury".
Shaftesbury at first demurred, for he knew that this probably meant that Palmerston was putting his hand in his
own pocket. There was further delay owing to the sudden
death on December 16th of Albert, the Prince Consort, one
whom Shaftesbury had never known intimately (who had?),
but whom he had recognized as one of his own way of
thinking and upon whose support he could always rely.
That same winter he heard of the passing of another old
friend and fellow knight-errant, Dr. Southwood Smith.
Death came very close that year.

In May 1862 he recorded in his Diary the acceptance of
the Garter. The fees had been "arranged": for Palmerston
knew full well that the inability to pay the thousand pounds
had been no excuse on Shaftesbury's part but veritable fact.
The Prime Minister was becoming increasingly anxious
about the agent Waters' behaviour, and had written to his

son-in-law, suggesting as tactfully as he could that he should let Palmerston's solicitors make a full enquiry. Perhaps because he was too busy thinking of other things, Shaftesbury took no immediate action, and there were yet further drainage contracts in the ensuing year, with the result that in 1863 the Earl was on the verge of bankruptcy. Waters was dismissed, Shaftesbury himself was the poorer by twelve thousand pounds, and a charge of embezzlement against his agent only produced endless lawsuits. Palmerston, instead of saying, " I told you so," sent Lady Shaftesbury five thousand pounds, his share, so he said, of " her sons' start in the world ". No wonder his friends loved him.

Pam, at long last, was growing old. He was eighty-one and still vigorous, still full of the joy of life. In the spring of 1865 he had a severe attack of gout, but on recovery he insisted on going down to Tiverton to meet his constituents as usual, for they liked to feel that their Prime Minister was kept well acquainted with their views on world affairs. Thence he went to his country home at Brocket where he was again unwell. He insisted on going out riding, caught a fresh chill, said " No " to his medicine like a spoilt child, and soon Evelyn Ashley had telegraphed for his mother and it was clear that the end was near. Shaftesbury followed his wife and was with Palmerston in his last hours, eagerly endeavouring by prayer and supplication to win from him a sign of his faith in the crucified Christ. He comforted himself that the drowsy breathing of his old friend was a sign of assent, as round about midday in the bright October sunshine Palmerston passed out of the world he had loved so well into the new adventures of the world beyond.

XI

"All God's Children . . ."

In the year 1847 at Manchester, the most enlightened town
in England (so its inhabitants thought), a man was sentenced
to ten years' transportation. He had been tried for man-
slaughter and the victim was a boy of seven. He was a
master-sweep and the child was his apprentice. The boy
had screamed and sobbed when his master sent him up the
chimney for the second time. But up he went, and down
he came unconscious. "The young devil is foxing," the
master cried and beat him to bring him round. The boy
recovered consciousness but died almost at once. The
master pleaded that few sweeps outside London did differ-
ently from himself. Good housewives insisted on having
their chimneys swept by chimney boys; these new-fangled
brushes were inefficient and dangerous. The chimneys
might fall down. Anyhow they scattered an enormous
amount of dust over the furniture and no good housewife
would let them be used in her rooms. So children of seven
were still sent up the smoky chimneys and at times, like
this poor little savage, they died. At Nottingham in 1850
a boy was jammed in the chimney above a blazing fire. A
man had to climb upon another's back to pull him out, too
late to live, from the inferno among the flues. Yes these
things happened in England, a Christian country, while
folk from all over Europe flocked to the Exhibition and
marvelled at her greatness, and housewives, equally unper-
turbed by the Exhibition and the murders, continued to use
chimney-boys because it was the correct thing to do, though
often they were kind-hearted ladies and gave them pennies
and pieces of cake, and made a point of enquiring if they
were perfectly willing to go up.

It made Shaftesbury's heart ache. All the forces against
which he had to struggle in his many crusades, the theories
of the industrialists, the capitalists' greed, the prejudice and

ignorance of the masses, the party ties of the politicians, proved more yielding than these stupid women. It had been comparatively easy to pass the necessary laws. The criminal brutality of the system had first been exposed as long ago as 1773 by that original and powerful personality Jonas Hanway, who wrote of the miserable condition of the sweeps in between helping Robert Raikes with his new experiment in Sunday schools and lessening the discomforts of mankind by inventing the umbrella. Since then various efforts had been made to mitigate the evil until in 1840, largely through the zeal of an insurance agent, Mr. Steven of the "Hand in Hand", the practice was definitely declared illegal in a Bill which Ashley enthusiastically supported. Nor was he content with political action; as always he expended himself in personal contact with the sufferers. He discovered that just behind his house in Brook Street a sweep lived who employed a child whom he refused to hand over except for an exorbitant sum. With Steven's help, Ashley unearthed the child's father, won his permission to educate the boy and bore him away in triumph to the Ragged School on Norwood Hill.

But he could not rescue every climbing boy, and time soon showed that vested interest, especially when exercised in the sacred name of property, could get round most laws on the statute book. The evil was gradually stamped out in London, but it persisted in the country. Landlords resented the necessity of modernizing their old crooked chimneys, and magistrates were slow to convict. There was nothing illegal in a sweep apprenticing a lad to his trade and letting him carry the brushes to the house concerned. It was then a simple matter for the boy, having taken the brushes inside, to do the job, in the old bad way. Only occasionally, as at Manchester and Nottingham, did things go wrong.

That was Shaftesbury's chance. Never once in the thirty-odd years of the struggle did he hear of a chimney boy's death but he publicized the case in the newspapers or in the House of Lords, till public opinion should at length be

stirred. One of his agents, Peter Hall, had an uncanny
knack of tracing down masters who were contravening the
law. He had once been a sweep himself. He too had his
child apprentice and sent him up to sweep the chimneys.
One day the child got into difficulties, could move neither
up nor down, was suffocated, and the wretched man himself
took down the small dead body from the narrow flue. He
never forgot; he never forgave himself, and he vented his
shame and horror on every master sweep that used a climbing boy through years of untiring search and ruthless
enquiry.

It was not only the danger to life which horrified Shaftesbury; it was the degrading conditions in which the boys
lived; the dirt and disease and appalling ignorance. They
were often barely six years old, " a nice trainable age ", and
their troubles began even before they climbed the chimney,
for it was the custom to harden their skin by rubbing it
with salt. While he was enjoying the pageantry of becoming
a Peer, Shaftesbury was also thinking of his sweeps, and his
first endeavours in the Upper House were to amend the law
on their behalf. But he had little success. A measure forbidding a sweep to have apprentices under sixteen passed
the Upper House but was dropped in the Commons; the
attempt was renewed in 1853, but a Select Committee reported against the Bill, and two more efforts in the succeeding years also failed. Everyone was thinking about the war;
with the nation at stake the fate of an odd child every now
and again was a paltry matter; and philanthropy was out
of fashion, " pitiful cant " one of Shaftesbury's opponents
called it. There was need for twenty more years of steady
propaganda. He persevered and in the next decade two
things helped him greatly. The one was the report of the
Children's Employment Commission, appointed at his instigation in 1861; the other was the publication, two years
later, of Charles Kingsley's *The Water Babies*.

It was only a fairy story, but such a story! It was the
age of large families, nurtured in the happy security of an
ordered nursery life, and in many a Victorian household

when the children trooped down to the drawing-room for the precious hour with Mamma, Mr. Kingsley's new book ("he's very advanced, my dear, but after all he *is* a clergy-man") would be read to the enthralled young listeners. "Mamma" maybe learnt as much as they, and somehow you couldn't after reading *The Water Babies* to the children allow the sweep to send a child up the nursery chimney next day! What an influence these Victorian novels had—what a weapon they were in the hands of men of feeling and prophetic power. The world had not grown blasé with too much reading then; the publication of a good novel was an event, and more perhaps than any other single force they moulded the opinion of the day, giving it a dynamic pur-pose all the stronger because the approach was through the emotions rather than the intellect. The latter was given food for thought—enough and to spare—by the Reports of the Parliamentary Commissions; and the process the one began the other completed till there came into existence, in regard to one social problem after another, a body of in-formed and potent opinion which men such as Normanby, Foster and Shaftesbury were able to canalize into effective parliamentary action.

But as for the sweeps, their troubles were not over. In 1864 a supplementary Act was passed, but once again it failed to be adequately administered. Three more children lost their lives—how many more suffered agonies in living! —before a vigorous press campaign enabled Shaftesbury in April 1875 to introduce a Bill, which subsequently became law. It enacted that every master sweep should be licensed annually, the licence being withheld if the law had been in any way contravened. Old Jonas Hanway had suggested a similar remedy a hundred years before. It is not a record of which the women of England can be proud; they should have cared less for their furniture and more for the welfare of other people's children.

Throughout these years Shaftesbury continually reminded himself that his task was not complete until every child in employment had become a " protected person ". In 1861 the second Commission of Enquiry was appointed, which resulted in the extension of the Factory Laws to six more industries, including the Potteries, where conditions had been particularly bad, but where the reformers had the cooperation of such enlightened employers as Minton and Wedgwood.

There was one large group of children, however, whose hard lot could not be so easily put right. These were the field gangs, employed mainly in the Eastern Midlands, weeding and gathering crops, hoeing turnips and planting potatoes under the direction of a gang-master often as foulmouthed and brutal as the butty of the mines. It was far harder to control the agriculturalists than it was to regulate hours in an organized industry, and it was not until the sixties, when there was a recrudescence of legislative activity and when, as a great landowner, he had come in closer contact with the bad state of affairs, that Shaftesbury moved for the Children's Employment Commission to enquire particularly into the condition of young people engaged in agriculture. Two years later, in 1867, the report was received. Upon this report Shaftesbury introduced a Bill prohibiting the employment in field work of all children under eight, or of girls under eleven, and forbidding any girl under eighteen to work in a public gang. Incredible as it may seem, in view of the evidence, the Bill was ardently opposed.

What evidence it was: evidence of depravity, immorality, hardships barely endurable that might well have shocked his fellow Peers into silence. The stories of the witnesses reminded one of the tales from the mills revealed before Sadler's Committee. One mother told how she had been persuaded to let her Susan, aged six, join her sisters at work. She walked the eight miles to Peterborough, worked all day in the fields (she was paid fourpence an hour) and was so tired that her sisters carried her home. She was ill next day so her mother did not send her again, but the sisters went on walking the sixteen miles to and fro and working a nine-and-a-half-hour day, and they were only eleven and thirteen.

More than twenty thousand children were employed in this way, and the report revealed that despite the advantages of fresh air and sunshine the children's death-rate at Wisbech was as high as that of Manchester. Rheumatism frequently developed before they reached their teens, yet physical discomfort was in some ways the least of their troubles. The gang-masters' brutality and the absence of any humanizing influence meant that those who survived grew up little better than savages, lusty young animals, the girls no different from the boys until on some lonely homeward road, or as they worked alone beneath a hedge, sexual desire flamed suddenly into life, and another frightened, ignorant waif of thirteen or fourteen was sent to the workhouse to have her baby.

None the less vested interest proved too strong for Shaftesbury. His Bill was withdrawn and the Government submitted another in its place, which merely provided for the licensing of gang-masters and laid down that a gang-mistress should also be employed. Six years later, when Gladstone was tackling every evil under the sun in his greatest ministry, Clare Read sponsored a measure which forbade the employment of any child under eight, at which age he could go to work provided he had reached the fourth standard in the local elementary school!

At the age of seventy, his powers of mind and body in no way impaired, Shaftesbury began yet another crusade to save the children of the brickyards. The facts and figures which he laid before the Peers were too convincing to brook opposition. Nearly thirty thousand young people between the ages of three and a half and seventeen were employed in the yards for a length of fourteen to sixteen hours a day. " I saw little children three parts naked tottering under the weight of wet clay, some of it on their heads and some on their shoulders. . . . When I approached they were so scared at seeing anything not like themselves that they ran screaming, as though something satanic was approaching."

This time he met with ready compliance, and the benefits of the Factory Acts were extended to these poor mites.

In such piecemeal ways were matters put right, without any large constructive action being taken to destroy the evils, material and spiritual, which reared their ugly heads beneath the thin veneer of Victorian convention and prosperity. Shaftesbury had done his part by establishing once for all the right and duty of the State to interfere ruthlessly with private individuals who were exploiting others for their own ends. But he was not the man to embody these actions into a philosophy of State control. He felt the need for some philosophy, some place for moral judgements in the conduct of public affairs. As a youth he had dreamed of a policy founded on the Bible. He corresponded in his later middle age with Cardinal Manning, discussing the possibility of concerted Christian action. But in the main his approach was *ad hoc*, and the value of what he did and what he was lay in that quality which his opponents called " his hopeless pertinacity ", his collection and use of facts, and his willingness to be content with small advances—and above all in his own Christian conscience, opposed " to the law of indifference and drift ". " This was his service to England," write the Hammonds at the conclusion of their biography, " not the service of a statesman with wide plans and commanding will, but the service of a prophet speaking truth to power in its selfishness and sloth."

Yet Shaftesbury would have been less than human if he did not regret at times that so much remained to be done. A man cannot fight indefinitely against destiny, which interferes remorselessly with his plans for the good of mankind, forcing him through the sorrow of personal bereavements, his own dwindling strength, the daily press of duties, into acquiescence with a lesser aim (or maybe it only seems a lesser aim), that of helping a few people instead of changing the world. Shaftesbury went steadily on. When the brickfield children were safe he did what he could for the acrobats; when he had helped the dress-

makers he made friends with the flower-women of Piccadilly. His interest lay increasingly along personal lines.
He felt, as many are coming to feel to-day, that no system
is perfect; every system like a machine is a potent force to
be used for good or evil according to the honesty or the
greed of the citizen who works it. He had preached incessantly that men could not be decent citizens under brutal
and filthy conditions; hence the need in the first place for
legislative action and sound administration. But neither
would this in itself suffice without a spiritual change of
heart which would enable them to put themselves and their
possessions low down in their scale of values. So while
he never relaxed his efforts at Westminster, he found increasingly his hope for the future in the Sunday services
and the work of the Ragged Schools.

In the months after Palmerston's death, when it was not
easy to disregard the blank not only in his private but in
his public life, it was to this aspect of his work that he
turned for consolation. In February 1866 he invited a
hundred or so homeless boys from the casual wards of the
London workhouses to join him at supper at St. Giles'
Refuge in Lincoln Inn Fields. After the meal he ques-
tioned them on how they lived. Twenty or thirty of them
had already been in prison; they ran about the streets by
day holding horses or cleaning boots and slept where and
how they could by night. "Supposing there were, in the
Thames, a big ship, large enough to contain a thousand
boys, would you like to be placed on board to be taught
trades or trained for the Navy and Merchant Service?" A
hundred hands and more shot up in an eager "Yes".
Supported by *The Times*, then as to-day a progressive
force when it wished to be, Shaftesbury approached the
Admiralty, and H.M.S. *Chichester* was granted for the
purpose. She was inaugurated as a training-ship in
December, and shortly afterwards H.M.S. *Arethusa* was also
put into service. The Merchant Navy, and England, have
had many a cause to be grateful, not least in the dark
days of the present war, for the boys of Shaftesbury's train-

ing-ships, and for the vision and determination that gave them their opportunity. Meanwhile, other such projects were set on foot: homes for girls at Sudbury and Ealing, and the farm at Bisley which bore Shaftesbury's name, where among the invigorating scent of the pines the good work could be continued of recreating God's children in His own image.

To-day, close upon a century later, in England's hour of crisis, the helping hand of " the good Earl " still stretches lovingly over London's children. From the Christmas Appeals of 1944 the smiling face of a boy looks out from the pages of *The Times*. His home destroyed, his parents killed by a bomb, so reads the text, he is happy now and safe " with The Shaftesbury Homes ". On the other pages of the journal there are records enough and to spare of suffering and brutality, yet as long as there is evil in the world, so long also will the work of Christian men endure, that ordinary folk may not lose their faith but may " see the goodness of the Lord in the land of the living ".

XII

Fulfilment

WHEN Palmerston died in 1865 Russell became Prime Minister, but in the following June the Government was defeated on the question of reform. Lord Derby succeeded, with Disraeli as leader of the Lower House, now able for the first time to fulfil the promise of Young England. For the next twenty years politics was an exciting duel between Dizzy, brilliant, ostentatious, shrewd, and Gladstone, slipping gradually from Galahad to Grand Old Man. Honours were divided. Disraeli, disliking the lower classes less than the bourgeoisie, extended the vote to the working man in 1867: three years later W. E. Forster carried his Education Act, which made possible the gradual extension of elementary education to all. The years of Gladstone's first ministry (1868-74), inspired largely by the writings of John Stuart Mill, marked a period of vitality and progress in politics as in things of the mind and of the body. The great giants of Victorian literature proclaimed England's ascendancy in the realm of letters, while in his factory by the Wandle, William Morris strove to prove that even industry might be a noble thing.

Shaftesbury, an old man, continued to work in Parliament for his chimney-boys and the extension of the Factory Acts, but he had little share in the new activities. Before the new measures and younger men of the next generation he felt " like an old tree in a forest half submerged by a mighty flood ". The Reform Act he disliked intensely, because he never regarded the vote as a right but always as a trust, and would have liked a distinction made between the ignorant and the intelligent working man. He felt no confidence that " out of this hecatomb of British traditions and British institutions there will arise the great and glorious Phœnix of a conservative democracy ", and he warned his fellow Peers that the masses were " not conservative of your

Lordships' titles and estates nor of the interests of the Established Church. They are living from hand to mouth, and in consequence they are very conservative of what they consider to be their own interests."

Shaftesbury's distrust of any attack upon the structure of society as he knew it was deeply rooted in his nature, fed by the aristocratic tradition and all the spiritual influences that centred round St. Giles. But one might have expected a more friendly attitude towards the spread of education, which he himself had so often urged. Yet even in this sphere he could not feel himself at one with the reformers. He distrusted the modern reliance on reason, the belief in man's perfectibility that the theory of evolution and the political philosophy of Mill triumphantly proclaimed. Through a long life of sacrifice and service he had found human effort so often unavailing, that he feared the temper of the new age, so sure of its own achievements; ". . . these social reforms, so necessary, so indispensable, seem to require as much of God's grace as a change of heart ". Education to him meant not so much the training of the mind as Christian teaching. "I stand up for God's word as the basis of education wherever I go." Hence his dislike of much in Forster's Education Bill which, partly because of the mutual antagonism of the different branches of the Christian Church, made religious teaching non-dogmatic and the character of elementary education in England mainly secular. To Shaftesbury this was particularly disastrous at a time when political power was passing into the hands of the working classes. He believed that only in the teaching of the Bible could one find the "principle of self-restraint which made a man respect himself and respect his neighbours ", a conclusion worth remembering as we start out to-day on the great venture of building a new world.

In one aspect, his distrust of Forster's Bill was linked with personal fears. He was afraid that the new system might find no place for the Ragged Schools, and he declared that his heart would break if they perished "under this all-conquering march of intellectual power ".

H

A happier figure than Shaftesbury the elderly Peer hating the " ballot ", ill at ease before the vigorous onrush of the Liberal Government, is Shaftesbury President of the Y.M.C.A., which he had helped to found, and whose gymnasium he opened with the proud reminder that he himself had been a good boxer in his youth. In how many corners of the world to-day have the clubs and canteens of the Y.M.C.A. proved themselves to be what he wished of them, " places where young men may find shelter and where they may learn the way of salvation and obtain courage and confidence to walk in it ".

It was in such realms of personal service, among the black-coated workers but still more among his beloved costers and the people of the streets, that Shaftesbury found his happiness in old age. He looked back, with affectionate tolerance, at the young man who had once hoped to be a scientist, then an author, and who now found himself at the end of a long life " simply an old man who has endeavoured to do his duty in that state of life to which it has pleased God to call him ". At seventy he was still erect, with few grey hairs, good eyesight and only a slight deafness. His feelings were as vivid and keen as in his youth, though he had schooled himself to be a little—only a little—less sensitive to affronts!

He still suffered from alternating moods of elation and despair, " intellectually not strong; over-anxious for success, over-fearful of failure . . . with a good deal of ambition and no real self-confidence ". He knew himself well by the age of seventy, and the only virtues he would claim were " feeling, perseverance and conviction ". Yet, none the less, with such remnants of power as he still possessed, he was ready with various projects to continue his public usefulness.

But a dark road lay before him. For a while his home life had been calm and happy. In 1869 there had been special cause for rejoicing when Anthony's son was born at St. Giles. The little village was all agog. A son and heir had not been born at St. Giles since the birth of the

first Lord Shaftesbury round about 1600. On the christen-
ing day " every cottage had flags and flowers . . . all the
people were exulting ". " He is one of us." " He is a fellow
villager." " We have now got a lord of our own." It was a
happy occasion, such as destiny is apt to give to mortals as
a perfect memory before the shadows close in upon a time
of suffering.

Such a time was ahead of Shaftesbury now. Constance
was ill and it was soon clear that the same agony lay ahead
as they had faced with Mary. During the greater part of
1870 and 1871 Lady Shaftesbury was on the Continent with
her daughter. Shaftesbury spent Christmas with them in
Italy, but there was snow instead of sun and lodging-houses
were less comfortable than home. Next winter they were
at Cannes, whence Shaftesbury returned in the new year of
1872 to a busy parliamentary session, mainly concerned with
the Ecclesiastical Courts Bill and meetings connected with
the Education Act. It was a troublesome, unsatisfactory
spring, yet further disturbed by rumours of discontent
among the agricultural workers. Shaftesbury poured out
his anxiety and preoccupation in long letters to his wife, and
turned for relaxation to the companionship of the two
grandchildren who were with him at Grosvenor Square,
Gigas, a small boy of five, and a little madam of three who
was nicknamed The Dwarf.

He was most usefully occupied this year with new housing
schemes, evolved by the Artisans Dwelling Company, which
he had initiated thirty years earlier. In 1867 a new society,
the General Dwellings Co. (Ltd.), had been formed to cope
with the rebuilding necessitated by certain slum-clearance
schemes. The two societies combined to build twelve
hundred houses for working men at Lavender Hill in
Battersea, a district less lovely than its name suggests but
with possibilities when men got together without thought
of personal gain. The new estate was named Shaftesbury
Park, and in August 1872 the Earl laid the foundation stone
of this new community which was to be run on a co-operative
system, and included not only dwelling-houses but shops,

schools, houses—the "neighbourhood unit" of the town-planning enthusiasts of to-day. "It is the only answer," wrote Shaftesbury, "to the insoluble problem how to improve the homes of the people. Charity cannot do it. The capitalists will not do it. The people themselves must do it, and here they have attempted it."

This was in August, just about the time that his wife and daughter reached home from the Continent. They went straight to Malvern, and there Lady Shaftesbury collapsed, worn out by many anxious years. She recovered sufficiently to return to London in late September, when to his dismay Shaftesbury was told that her illness was dangerous. On October 15th she died. The saddest entry in the Diary are the words her husband wrote on the same evening in his cruel loneliness: "To-night will be a terrible event. For the first time I must omit in my prayers the name of my precious Minnie." His stern Protestantism did indeed, on this occasion, exact a terrible price. "A wife as good, as true and as deeply beloved as God in His undeserved mercy ever gave a man." He buried her at Wimborne St. Giles and tried to continue her task of looking after Constance. With his youngest son Cecil to help him they set out for Mentone. There he grappled with his own sorrow, nursed his daughter through a last bout of illness, and in December watched her die, happy to be released from the suffering flesh.

The New Year saw him in harness again. The first meeting he attended was at the Costermongers' Club. To these simple folk, living close to the basic facts of life—love and death and fear—it was easy to show one's grief, untrammelled by the repressions of the sophisticated world. It was comforting to feel their honest sympathy. He had feared at first that his loss would cripple him. He had relied so much on his wife's quiet affection in the background of his life. But he found that his sorrow was a key to open the hearts of men. He could share their griefs as never before; he had a right to help them now. It was no longer a question of patronage, of one outside who could not really understand. When he spoke at the Ragged Schools Flower

Show in May Shaftesbury put into words what he was dimly feeling: "The great and final Garden of Paradise is only to be approached through the Garden of Gethsemane." A voice from the crowd cried out, "That is the best thing you have said."

So, during the course of the next few years, the old Earl seemed to enjoy a renewal of energy and hope. Old schemes went ahead: new ideas were put into practice. Most successful of the latter was an arrangement for issuing loans to the young women who appeared in different guises in the London streets, selling flowers or fruit or watercress or keeping coffee-stalls in winter. He called it the Emily Loan Fund, and over a period of years during which close on one thousand loans were issued, less than fifty pounds were lost. Many a girl was thus enabled to tide over bad times, and maybe to set herself up with a coffee-stall. He loved such work, and the visits to Whitechapel, where his numerous trips up and down the back streets were distinguished by the fact that he did not forget the promises he made to all and sundry. After one such visit he wrote to his companion, Mr. Orsman of the Costermongers' Mission, "Do not forget the woman who made the Braces. We promised her something. . . . Your missionaries must talk to the poor Cabinet Maker and *pray* with him. He is not hardened. Let him have what he wants in his necessity. . . . I have sent you a book for the two sons of the woman (spectacles) and the paralytic husband. Also picture cards, as I promised to the little girl. . . ."

Such excursions were luxuries. He did not neglect the less congenial duties such as attendance at the House of Lords, even though he described it as "that aquarium, full of cold-blooded life". In May 1875 the Government brought in the Artisans Dwelling Bill and he supported it ably, though he was convinced that the problems arising from slum clearance had not yet begun to be mastered. Ten years later a Commission was appointed to go into the whole Housing Question and the first witness called was Shaftesbury.

There was still much of the crusader in him, and he recognized a fellow enthusiast in a certain M.P. for Derby who was making himself heard and felt to the annoyance and discomfort of the Government. This was Samuel Plimsoll, who was working in the cause of the sailors of the Mercantile Marine. His anger was specially directed towards "coffin-ships", as he called the overloaded cargo vessels, which so often failed to return to port. It made his blood boil that the crews should lose their lives and the owners draw the insurance. It was easy to enlist Shaftesbury's sympathy and support. In the usual British way a committee was formed, with Shaftesbury as its Chairman, to put pressure on the Government to pass a Protection Act while a fuller enquiry was being made by means of a Royal Commission. On March 24th, 1873, there was a meeting of London workmen in Exeter Hall to support Plimsoll. "Very full, singularly enthusiastic, and yet prudent and judicious," Shaftesbury reported. But " judicious " was not the word to apply to Plimsoll himself. He was hot-blooded and erratic; it was no easy matter being his Chairman. Shaftesbury was very anxious. "He will ruin himself and the cause by his violence. He says what he believes and believes what he says, and he will take no man's advice. . . . His great and true facts will all be neutralized by his small and inaccurate statements." In 1875 a Merchant Shipping Bill was brought forward by the Government. Plimsoll thought it did not go far enough, but agreed to accept it. In July, however, Disraeli stated that he was proceeding no further in the matter that session. Plimsoll lost his temper. He walked down the centre of the House, pointing his finger at the shocked M.P.s and crying: " I will unmask the villains who have sent brave men to death." Even Shaftesbury was scandalized! He urged Plimsoll to apologize and eventually the latter agreed. Like most hot-tempered men, it was soon over—and the cause was not injured; in fact most ordinary folk felt that a few straight words, barbed with righteous anger, had not been out of place. Next year the Merchant Shipping Bill was passed, Shaftesbury advising and curbing

his impetuous friend to the last. Henceforward merchant
ships sailed from British ports marked with the Plimsoll
line, which line had to remain above sea-level and guaran-
teed that the vessel was not overloaded so as to endanger
the lives of the crew. Samuel turned his attention to cattle-
boats, and Shaftesbury to the state of industry in India.
Thank God for the crusaders!

India had been the first subject upon which, in his
twenties, the young reformer had concentrated his attention. The changes and chances of politics had driven him
elsewhere, until now, in his old age, he returned to his first
interest. People were thinking about India in 1876 because
of Disraeli's flamboyant gesture in transforming his Queen
into an Empress. On February 17th he introduced a Bill
which should enable Her Majesty to style herself " Empress
of India ". Two days after the second reading in March
Shaftesbury was invited to visit Windsor, an honour he
had not enjoyed for twenty years. If she meant to ask his
advice about accepting the title she changed her mind,
perhaps the sight of his uncompromising rectitude con-
firmed her suspicion that he would not approve. If she
thought her graciousness would make him change his
mind she was less shrewd than was her wont. At the end
of the month he gave notice of an address to the Crown,
praying Her Majesty not to take the title of Empress, and
on April 3rd he moved an amendment to this effect. He
saw that the future of the British Empire lay in something
other than imperialism. As to the title he said, " It will
have an air, military, despotic, offensive and intolerable
alike in the East and West of the Dominions of England."
His final words were a fitting close to the parliamentary
career of one who had upheld the cause of the unfortunate
at the cost of office and influence and much that men hold
dear. " A time may come when, after a long course of
happy rule, we may surrender India to natives, grown into
a capability of self-government. Our posterity may then
see an enlargement of the glorious spectacle we now witness, when India shall be added to the roll of free and

independent powers that wait on the mother country and
daily rise up and call her blessed." He lost his motion, of
course, but in the few years left to him he thought much
of India and our responsibility for its population, and in
1879 he again moved an address to the Crown, urging that
action should be taken to regulate the work of women and
children in the Indian cotton mills. It seemed as if the
vigour of his youth had been restored to him as he spoke,
reliving his experiences of the thirties, the terrible sights
he had seen in the north before the Factory Acts were
passed, the improvement already made which he claimed
as a right for India also. " No climate can enable infants
to do the work of adults or turn suffering women into mere
steam engines. Creed and colour, latitude and longitude,
make no difference in the essential nature of man." It was
his swan song and not an unworthy one.

The last years passed quietly. Scarcely serenely—for
serenity was the one gift denied to Shaftesbury. Perhaps
he cared too much. Life still appeared to him as a
trial of strength, a wrestle with the forces of evil. " Every
day brings a scene like mounting the Rigi," he wrote to
Hilda, his unmarried daughter and faithful companion,
who was away on a visit to Evelyn's invalid wife. " At each
ten minutes you fancy you have reached the highest point,
and when you have reached the highest point you see a
hundred points inaccessibly above you. So it is, so it will
be to the end of the world. The completion of things is
reserved for our blessed Lord." But he found it hard at
times to achieve such resignation. As recurrent pain and
increasing difficulty in movement warned him of the end
he worried—not for himself but for the suffering world.
As he worked feverishly for this good cause or that: the
acrobat children, the welfare of young girls, the suppres-
sion of the opium trade; or grappled with fresh problems
arising from a new Lunacy Act; took Chair upon Chair at
endless meetings, often in great personal discomfort;
quarrelled with the Salvation Army and grieved at the
death of that dear enemy Dr. Pusey, his cry was not, as it

well might have been, for rest but for reprieve: " I cannot bear to leave the world with all the misery in it."

There were happier occasions. In 1880, when the centenary of Sunday schools was celebrated, he went down to Gloucester to unveil a statue to Robert Raikes. His old friend Haldane went with him; no two men could more fittingly express a nation's thanks to the pioneer who, in the gloomy labyrinths of eighteenth-century formalism, had lit the beacon of live Christian teaching. Next spring Shaftesbury celebrated his own eightieth birthday, and the Ragged School Union honoured their President in a great meeting at the Guildhall, while letters and presents poured in from every corner of England; tributes from the Archbishop of Canterbury, paper flowers from children he had helped. A year or so later he attended another birthday celebration, when Spurgeon, the great preacher, reached the age of fifty. " I want old-fashioned Evangelical doctrine to be identified with the event," Spurgeon had written in asking him to come. " A wonderful sight, nearly if not quite seven thousand adult, enthusiastic souls crammed even to suffocation by way of audience." Shaftesbury, presiding, was seized with appalling nervousness, stumbled into speech and excelled himself.

During these last years his physical state and his spirits fluctuated greatly. Christmas of '82 saw him happy at St. Giles with all his family about him, except Anthony, whose wife Margaret and the babies took his place. With Anthony and Evelyn both married and in Parliament, Shaftesbury could rest secure that the family tradition would be carried on. " Vea " was married also, to an Irish Peer, Lord Templemore. Her father had recently visited her in her new home, but he did not think much of Dublin. This Christmas reunion was a great joy to him for he was conscious that it might well be the last. He thanked God for all his home had meant to him as they took Communion together, Evelyn, Lionel, Cecil, Vea, Hilda and Margaret.

He lived for three more years. There were days when

he declared himself "fit to fight the Devil and all his angels". There were others, such as his eighty-fourth birthday, "terrible for pain and irritation". Life narrowed down into anxious forebodings as to whether he could fulfil the next engagement, and relief and gratitude when he had been enabled to do so. He mustered sufficient energy to help the cause of Jewish refugees from Russia and to attend the first anniversary of the Society for the Prevention of Cruelty to Children. And he tried hard to get to the Flower Girls' Tea-Party which he had promised to attend.

When he could not go out he sat in his study, worrying because it was wet on the day of "my poor little children's annual outing. They must have been sadly disappointed they could not roll on the wet grass." Or, in happier mood, he displayed to visitors the picture on his desk of a "fine lady" who once, years ago, had been brought to his doorstep in rags. And then, if the visitor still lingered, he would be shown some of the presents the children had given Shaftesbury. "I have had slippers and stockings, I have had shoes and waistcoats and bed linen too, coverlets, counterpanes, well, everything but a coat, and they gave me such a quantity of writing-paper that I assure you it was enough for all my own correspondence for a month."

It was hot and tiring in London in that summer of 1885, and in July his family persuaded him to go to Folkestone. Vea came over to help Hilda to look after him. They helped him with his letters, which were still a trouble to him, and shared his quiet enjoyment of the autumn evenings.

A chill hastened the end and his strength failed rapidly. He worried a little about being away from home, but except for that he lay at peace, only asking each morning for someone to read him the twenty-third Psalm. On October 1st he died, and afterwards they recalled that the last thing he had said was, "Thank you."

The authorities wished him to be buried in the Abbey, but he himself had said St. Giles. That was where he belonged, all that was mortal of him. But he himself belonged to England and to the people he had helped. A man stood in the London crowd, a *crêpe* band sewn upon his ragged coat. " Our Earl's gone," he cried, " God Almighty knows he loved us and we loved him. We shan't see his likes again."

So ends the story of a crowded life, full of the business of doing good. True, it was a Victorian life, devoted largely to that " ambulance " work which the reformers of to-day decry. He was Patron—and gloried in it—of a hundred good causes and the day of patronage is over. Yet one may admit all this, admit that patronage is hateful, that Ragged Schools have given place to " equal opportunities for all ", that a new social system is required, not the piecemeal betterment of the workers' conditions—and yet the fact remains that Shaftesbury did not only patronize. He cared. The wretchedness of folk kept him awake at night. They were men and women to him, whose lives mattered, for whose well-being he was personally responsible. There is need always for a Plimsoll's impetuous wrath, for Oastler's zeal, for Arnold's " sweetness and light "—and there is not much shortage to-day of informed opinion, self-discipline and party fervour. But there is need also— perhaps more than ever in this age of statistics and the socialized state—for the man and woman who care, who are made hideously uncomfortable by the ugliness of much of life, who go out to do something, however inconvenient to themselves and others it may be, and do not, like Vol- taire's well-meaning gentry, " eat their supper and forget ".

Perhaps this is the first and last thing to remember about him, for those who try to help their fellows through any motive less than love, sooner or later stumble in the dark. Shaftesbury had his limitations, many of them : yet he changed for the better the lives of millions, achieving the impossible by hard work and importunity and prayer. Private prayer each day in his own room, public worship on Sunday at St. Giles or at the church in Portman Square, regular Communion, all the ordinary spiritual exercises of a Christian that he took for granted, and that to-day it is so easy to neglect. No man was more conscious of the pressure of daily affairs, but to him it would have been as sensible to endeavour to work the machines without that motive-power over which his north-country friends concerned themselves so closely, as to drive the human spirit along the road of progress without the aid of God, through prayer and worship. In this faith he went forward, giving God the glory and passing on to the next job, doing at every stage and in all circumstances what appeared to be right! If it was his charity, in the true sense of that word, which enriched his life, and his steady reliance upon God's grace which empowered him, it was this staunch integrity of his which guided him aright amid the conflicting temptations and perplexities of this world.

He did so much. If one man, not brilliant nor over-confident, could do so much, what could the world accomplish if it set itself the same rule of living? Shaftesbury's career is impressive regarded merely as an account of progress made in every branch of social welfare and humanitarian activity. Regarded as a manifestation of the Holy Spirit of God working in the heart of man, it humbles and exalts us to-day as we look out upon a tired and puzzled world. Down the years, from an age already remote, the stern unbending figure of the Great Victorian bids us take courage and be content so long as we can see merely the next step forward. There is no end to the journey, no Utopia here and now; it is not for us to reach the summit of the Rigi. Yet no soldier of Christ can fall out by the way. Shaftesbury's words, those of an old campaigner, sound across the century, "By everything true, everything holy, you are your brother's keeper." To-day an army of men of goodwill eagerly say " Amen ". May God grant them as they go forward along an uncharted road, the vision and patience He gave to those who have gone before, the Faith that moves mountains and the Love that casteth out fear.

Index

Rouen, 151
Routine, 27; *and see* Bureaucracy; Sentries
Rovno, 286
RSHA, xvii, (52), 149, 165, (205), 215
RSS, xvii, 133, 136–7
Rubber, 48
Rudnicki, K. S., 293n, 297n
Ruhr, 234, 279, 314n
Rumour, 30, 33, 57–8
Rundstedt, G. von, 258, 309
Ruritania, 147
RUSIĴ, cited, xvii, 26n, 139, 279, 282
Russell, D., 171
Russia, 12, 15, 33, 146, 151–2, 173, 191, 196, 202, 232, 286–92, 315–16; *and see* USSR
Ruthenia, 199
'Rutland', *see* Blommaert, J. de
RVV, group, xvii, 261, 267

Saarland, 211
Sabotage, 8–10, 23–4, **43–9**, 67, 91, 98, 137–8, 154, 159, 161, 165, 170–1, 177, 180–2, 196, 201, 232, 234, 250–2, 274–7, 282; assessed, **313–15**
Sadi-Kirschen, G. ('Fabian'), 269
Safe houses, 14, 41, 118
St Cast, 39
St Etienne, 251
'St Jacques', *see* Duclos, M.
St-Marcel, 55
St Nazaire, 38, 58, 209, 247n
St-Valéry-en-Caux, (137), 244
Salazar, A. de O., 75, 79, (231)
'Sally', *see* Strugo
Salò, 225–6, 228
Salonika, 177, 180–1
Sanatescu, gen., 172–3
Sant, F. van 't, 262, 264
Sarajevo, 50, 150, 187
Saraphis, S. 180
Sardinia, 29, 222n
Sartre, J-P., 60, (239)
SAS, *see* Army, British
Satellite states of nazi Germany, 2, 3, 23, 42, 47, 76, 128, 169–73, 188–9, 204–9, 284, 286
'Saturday', *see* Neave
Saunders, H. St G., cited, 162n
Savill, M., cited, 118 and n
Savoy, 112, 122, 235, 251, 252
Sayers, Dorothy, cited, 108
SBS, *see* Army, British
Scandinavia, 79, 83, 139, 271–3, 283; *an see* Denmark; Finland; Iceland; Norway; Sweden
Scavenius, E., 273
Schacht, H., 169, 302
Scheldt, river, 258, 261, (268)
Schellenberg, W., 141
Schiller, (J. C.) F. von, 266
Schlesinger, A. M. jr, 51n, 63n, 142
Schnabel, R., 251 and n

Scholl, H. and S., 302–3
Schoolteachers, 19–20, 40, 60, 81–2, 88, 282
Schrage, W. B., 262–3
Schreieder, J., 264–7
Schulze-Gaevernitz, G. von, 218
Schuschnigg, K. von, 210–11
Schwarz, B. I., cited, 85n
Schweinfurt, 23
'Scientist', *see* Baissac, C. de
Scotland, 30, 46, 117, 183, 279–80, 282, 284–5, 314
Scott, K. A. V., 175
SD, xvii, 19, 20, 52, 63–9, 88–9, 110, 136, 140, 149, 165, 205, 215, 220, 240, 245, 248–50, 263–7, 289, 300n
Sea landings, 17, 54, 56, 109, **115–18**, 159, 177, 180, 182–3, 185, 187, 194, 197, 225, 227–8, 252, 261–2, 277, 280–1
Seailles, P., 250
Seailles, S., 249
Sebastopol, 151, 253
'Second World War', 3 and n; *and passim*
Secret ink, 99
Secret services, 7–10, 15–16, 29, 30, 41, 56, 81, 97–8, **132–49**, 287–8; *and see* Counter-espionage, and particular services
Security, 8, 28–9, 36, 41–2, 62, **63–9**, 81, 86, 123, 158–9, 162–3, 203, 247–8, 256n, 259–60, 292, 296, 312
— checks, *see* Wireless
Sehmer, J., 208
Sein, Ile de, 116
Selborne, Lord, 138–9, 159
Selby, N., 196
Self-government, 72–3
Sentries, 37–9, 43, 47, 49, 51–2, 161, 243, 262, 291, 315
Separation, clandestine, 63, 99
—, marital, 82
Serbia, 150, 165, 168, 183, **186–98**
Sergueiev, Lily, 230
Sète, 252
Seton-Watson, C., 221n
Seton-Watson, H., 191n, 193, 200n, 208n
Seton-Watson, R. W., 186n, 203
Sevenet, H. P., 250, 252
Seyss-Inquart, A., 83, 261, 263
SFIO, 83
Shakespeare, W., cited, 75
Shannon, R. T., cited, 173n
Shaw, G. Bernard, 83
'Shelley', *see* Yeo-Thomas
Shetland, 117, 280
Shipping, 273, 277, 279; *and see* Ships
Ships,
  Audacious, 58
  Bismarck, 284
  caiques, 38, 117, 177–8
  feluccas, 38, 117–18
  Fidelity, 117, 229, 232, 244
  fishing boats, 116–18, 280
  Gneisenau, 241

Vomécourt, Philippe de, 42, 249
Vomécourt, Pierre de, (241), 249
Voronezh, 200
Voroshilov, K. Y., (8)
Vosges, 252
Vrinten, A. J. J., (136, 234, 241, **262**)

W committee, xviii, 132–3
Waals, A. van der, 265
Waffen-SS, 40, 55n, 64n, 65, 149, 193,
    203, 237, (251), 252, 254, 263, 268,
    290–1, **293–4**, 314–17
Wagner, H., 169n
Waibel, M., 220
Walker, D. E., 96, 170, 190, 233, 260
Wallace, G. C., 149
'Wally, Little', *see* Hradecky
Wandsworth, 134
War,
    Anglo-Irish, 4, 7, 48, 57, 129, 183n, 236
    Arab-Israeli (1948), 162–3
    Balkan (1912–13), 168–9, 173–4, 176
    civil, 22, 61–3
    —, Albanian, 184–5
    —, American, 72
    —, German (1866), 169, 198
    —, Greek, 181–2, 189
    —, Russian, 70–1, 90, 92
    —, Spanish, 1–2, 7, 35, 79, 83, 85,
        92–3, 190–1, 221–2, **230–1**, 239,
        257n, 272
    —, Yugoslav, 188–92, 194–5
—, cold, 62–3, 73, 74 and n, 218–19, 289
—, eighty years', 261
—,
    Franco-Austrian (1859), 77, 220–1
    Franco-Prussian (1870–1), 50, 129, 210,
        234–5, 306
    Greco-Italian (1940–1), 2, 177
    multilateral, 70–1, 156, 194, 291–2, 295
    naming of, 2n, 3n, 4n
    of independence, American, 73, 160,
        180
    personal base of, 71; *and see* Casualties
    right to levy, 5–6
—, world, 3n
— —, of 1792–1815, 3, 5, 14, 36–7,
    235, 306
— —, of 1914–18, 1, 4 and n, 28, 50, 58,
    62–3, 118, 129, 134–5, 138–9, 150,
    162–4, 169, 176, 198, 210, 213, 214,
    217–18, 227, 232, 236, 254, 270, 287
— —, of 1939–45, *passim*
Warmbrunn, W., cited, 259n
Warsaw, 55, 56, 57, 121, 152, 208, 251,
    292, **294–300**
Washington, 8, 25, 27n, 62–3, 73, **141–4**,
    218–19, 226, 233, 273
Wassmuss, W., 129, 163
Watt, D. C., cited, 307n
Waugh, E., 59, 88, 317
Wavell, Sir A. P., earl, 28n, 119, 127,
    157, 305–6

Weapons, 25–6
    Abrasive grease, 43, 131
    Artillery, 57, 125, 130, 196, 314
    Brens, 16, 203, 281
    Caltrops, 31, 48
    Explosives, 16, 45–8, 277, 282, 303,
        313–14
    Fuses, 47; *and see* Time pencils *below*
    Grenades, 46, 49, 60, 206
    Incendiaries, 45–6
    Knives, 48n, 49, 55
    Machine guns, 55, 130
    Mines, 45, 47–8, 245
    Mortars, 130
    Pistols, 40, 49, 51–2, 55
    Rifles, 51 and n, 55
    Stens, 10, 80–1, **129–30**, 206, 267
    Sub-machine guns, other, 10, 57, **129**,
        241
    Supply, q.v.
    Time pencils, 10, 45, 53
    Tyrebursters, 31
    Welrods, 45
    Wire, 49
    Wireless, q.v.
Weather, 17, 24, 27, 122–3, 204, 234,
    271, 272
Wehrmacht, 1–3, 25, 173, 177, 190, 260,
    301, 307; *and see* its components:
    Army, German; Luftwaffe; Navy,
    German; OKW; *Waffen-SS*
Weimar, 302; *and see* Concentration
    camps, nazi, Buchenwald
Weinzierl, Erika, cited, 212n
Weissberg, A., 144
Weizmann, C., 163n
Welrod, *see* Weapons
Welwyn, 45
Wenceslas, 202n
Westminster, *see* London
Wheatstone, Sir C., 108n
Wheeler-Bennett, (Sir) J. W., cited, 186n,
    301
'White Rabbit', *see* Yeo-Thomas
White Russia, *see* Byelorussia
White, R. T., *see* Hawes
Wilhelm II, German emperor, 153, 176
Wilhelmina, queen of the Netherlands,
    260, 262n, 264
Willetts, H. T., 295
Williams, E., 36
Wilno, *see* Vilna
Wilson, H. M. (Lord), 158–9
Wilson, (Sir) J. H., 75
Wilson, J. S., 281
Wilson, W., 169
Wingate, O., 53, 54, 157, 162
Winning side, 71, 75
Wint, G., *see* Calvocoressi
Winterbotham, F. W., 269n, 308
Wireless, clandestine, 14–15, 30, 41, 60,
    80–1, **102–9**, 133, 136–7, 168, 171, 175,
    190, 205, 213–16, 243, 244, 246, 256,
    260, **276**, 294, **296**

AFRICA IN HISTORY   Basil Davidson   £1.50
A complete introduction to the history of the 'Dark Continent'.
Illustrated.

THE ALCHEMISTS   F. Sherwood Taylor   £1.25
Before it became regarded as a branch of the occult, alchemy was in
the forefront of the search for human knowledge and led to the
founding of modern chemistry. Illustrated.

ANATOMY OF THE SS STATE
Helmut Krausnick and Martin Brozat   60p
The inside story of the concentration camps, 'probably the most
impressive work on the Nazi period ever to appear'. THE TIMES
EDUCATIONAL SUPPLEMENT.

ART AND THE INDUSTRIAL REVOLUTION
Francis D. Klingender   £1.50
One of the most original and arresting accounts of the impact of the
new industry and technology upon the landscape of England and the
English mind. 'There is no book like it.' *John Betjeman*. Illustrated.

ASPECTS OF THE FRENCH REVOLUTION
Alfred Cobban   75p
The origins of the Revolution, the role of the Enlightenment, *The
Parlement*, the diamond necklace affair. 'A tremendous and enviable
achievement of scholarship.' *David Thomson*.

THE BORGIAS   Michael Mallett   90p
The rise and fall of one of the most notorious families in
European history: Legends of poisoning, incest, and political
contrivance. Illustrated.

*All these books are available at your local bookshop or newsagent, or can be
ordered direct from the publisher. Just tick the titles you want and fill in the
form below.*

Name ....

Address ....

....

Write to Paladin Cash Sales, PO Box 11, Falmouth, Cornwall TR10 9EN

Please enclose remittance to the value of the cover price plus:

UK: 18p for the first book plus 8p per copy for each additional book
ordered to a maximum charge of 66p

BFPO and EIRE: 18p for the first book plus 8p per copy for the next 6
books, thereafter 3p per book

Overseas: 20p for first book and 10p for each additional book

*Granada Publishing reserve the right to show new retail prices on covers, which
may differ from those previously advertised in the text or elsewhere.*